ENGLISH FURNITURE
1760-1900

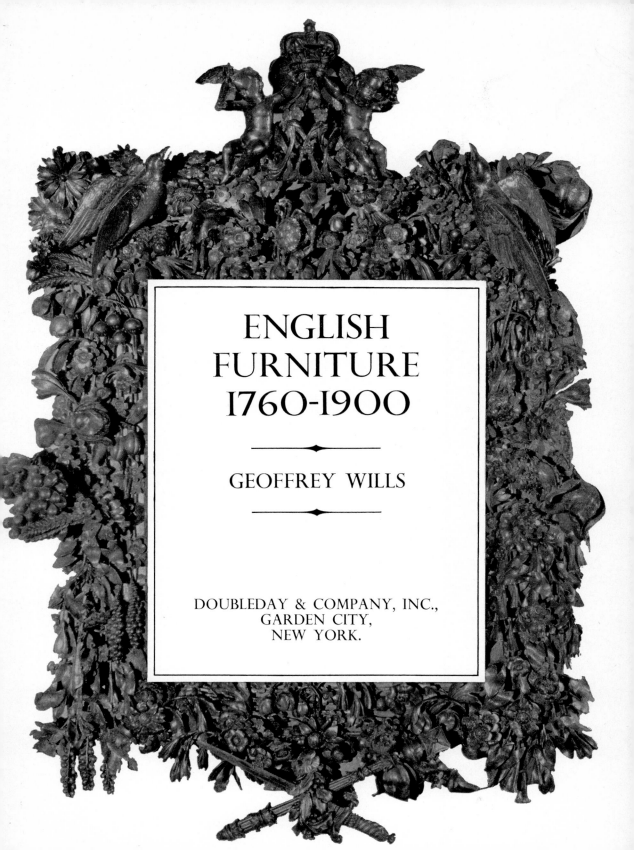

ENGLISH
FURNITURE
1760-1900

GEOFFREY WILLS

DOUBLEDAY & COMPANY, INC.,
GARDEN CITY,
NEW YORK.

Other Books in this Series

ENGLISH AND IRISH GLASS (1968)
by Geoffrey Wills
SBN 85112 117 9

ENGLISH POTTERY AND PORCELAIN (1969)
by Geoffrey Wills
SBN 85112 145 4

ANTIQUE FIREARMS (1969)
by Frederick Wilkinson
SBN 85112 164 0

EDGED WEAPONS (1970)
by Frederick Wilkinson
SBN 85112 171 3

BATTLE DRESS (1970)
(A Gallery of Military Style and Ornament)
by Frederick Wilkinson
SBN 85112 172 1

BRITISH GALLANTRY AWARDS (1971)
by P. E. Abbott and J. M. A. Tamplin
SBN 85112 173 X

ENGLISH FURNITURE, 1550–1760 (1971)
by Geoffrey Wills
SBN 85112 174 8

THE UNIVERSAL SOLDIER (1971)
edited by Martin Windrow and Frederick Wilkinson
SBN 85112 176 4

GUINNESS SUPERLATIVES LTD.
1971
SBN 85112 175 6

Published in Great Britain by
GUINNESS SUPERLATIVES LTD.,
2 CECIL COURT, LONDON ROAD, ENFIELD, MIDDLESEX
Printed in 10pt. Century Series 227
by McCorquodale Printers Limited, London.
Monotone and 4-colour half-tone blocks by Gilchrist Bros. Ltd., Leeds.

ACKNOWLEDGEMENTS

THESE two volumes, which cover the history of English furniture between 1550 and 1900, could not have been written and illustrated without the generous assistance of many people. Often, help of one kind and another was urgently needed at short notice, but without fail it was quickly forthcoming; this occurring in many instances despite a hiatus in postal services.

I am grateful to the owners of furniture who kindly allowed me access to their homes so that the numerous photographs of their possessions, hitherto unpublished and mostly acknowledged at their request as 'Private collection', might be taken; to Mr and Mrs J. K. des Fontaines for photographs; to the officials of the National Trust at various mansions who not only permitted photography but did all they could to assist the work; to Alison Kelly who lent me her treasured copy of Mrs Panton's *From Kitchen to Garret*; to L. G. G. Ramsey, F.S.A., Editor of *The Connoisseur*, for the loan of photographs of pieces in his own possession and others from the files of the magazine; to Christopher Gilbert, Keeper, Temple Newsam House, Leeds, for arranging photography and providing details of pieces in his care; to H. L. Douch, Curator, County Museum, Truro, who drew my attention to the Mohun and Pendarves inventories published for the first time in the companion to this, *English Furniture 1550–1760*, and who transcribed them from the originals in the Cornwall County Record Office; to the undermentioned dealers who lent valuable photographs:

Mary Bellis, Hungerford, Berks.   (Mrs M. Bellis)
H. Blairman & Sons, London   (Mr George Levy)
H. W. Keil, Ltd., Broadway, Worcs.   (Mr H. W. Keil)
John Keil, Ltd., London   (Mr J. M. M. Keil)
Mallett & Son, Ltd., London   (Mr R. E. de Zoete)
Pelham Galleries, Ltd., London   (Mr H. W. Rubin);

also to the undermentioned firms of auctioneers who permitted the use of photographs:

Christie's, London
Phillips', London
Sotheby's, London
Bearnes & Waycotts, Torquay, Devon
King & Chasemore, Pulborough, Sussex
Parke-Bernet Galleries, Inc., New York City.

Finally, I thank my publishers, their managing Editor, Frank Mason, their series editor, Martin Windrow, and their Editorial Assistant, Sue Beaty for their patient co-operation.

G.W.

LONDON 1763

The St. Martin's Lane area, showing the locations of cabinet-makers
and others, with the dates when occupancy began.

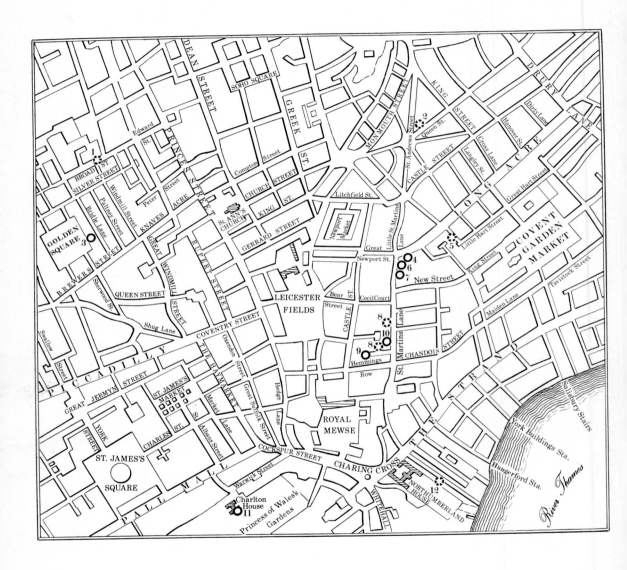

KEY

1 Ince & Mayhew, 1759
2 Thomas Johnson, 1755
3 George Cole, *c.* 1745
4 William Hallet, 1752
5 T. Chippendale, 1749
6 Vile & Cobb, 1750
7 Thomas Chippendale, 1754
8 ? St. Martin's Lane Academy
9 Peter's Court
10 John Channon, *c.* 1737
11 Charlton House
12 T. Chippendale, 1752

All sites are approximate, but those marked with a dotted ring refer to a
street in general and not to a particular building in it.

CONTENTS

BIBLIOGRAPHY

Lɪsᴛ of principal books cited and consulted
(Published in London unless otherwise stated)

Elizabeth Aslin
  19th Century English Furniture, 1962.
Arthur T. Bolton
  The Architecture of Robert and James Adam, 2 vols.,
  1922.
Oliver Brackett
  Thomas Chippendale, 1923.
The Cabinet-Maker's Assistant, 1853, reprinted as *The
  Victorian Cabinet-Maker's Assistant*, 1970.
Thomas Chippendale
  The Gentleman and Cabinet-Maker's Director, 1754,
  3rd edition, 1762, reprinted 1957.
Anthony Coleridge
  Chippendale Furniture, 1968.
H. M. Colvin
  A Biographical Dictionary of English Architects,
  1954.
*Autobiography and Correspondence of Mary Granville,
  Mrs Delany*: ed. Lady Llanover, 6 vols., 1861–2.
Charles L. Eastlake
  Hints on Household Taste, 1868.
Ralph Edwards and Margaret Jourdain
  Georgian Cabinet-Makers, 3rd edition, 1955.
Ralph Fastnedge
  Sheraton Furniture, 1962.
C. H. Gibbs-Smith
  The Great Exhibition of 1851, 1950.
John Gloag
  Mr. Loudon's England, Newcastle upon Tyne, 1970.
*Great Exhibition, 1851: Official Descriptive and Illus-
  trated Catalogue*, 3 vols., 1851, supplementary vol.,
  1853.
Eileen Harris
  The Furniture of Robert Adam, 1963.
Helena Hayward
  Thomas Johnson and English Rococo, 1964.
Ambrose Heal
  London Furniture Makers 1660–1840, 1953.
A. Hepplewhite and Co.
  The Cabinet-Maker and Upholsterer's Guide, 1788,
  3rd edition, 1794, reprinted 1969.
William Ince and John Mayhew
  The Universal System of Household Furniture, 1762,
  reprinted 1960.
Simon Jervis
  Victorian Furniture, 1968.
Margaret Jourdain
  Regency Furniture, 1934, revised edition, 1949.
Alison Kelly
  Decorative Wedgwood, 1965.

J. C. Loudon
  *Encyclopaedia of Cottage, Farm and Villa Archi-
  tecture and Furniture*, 1833.
  Loudon's Furniture Designs, 1970.
Percy Macquoid and Ralph Edwards
  The Dictionary of English Furniture, 2nd edition,
  revised by Ralph Edwards, 3 vols., 1954.
Robert Manwaring
  The Cabinet and Chair-Maker's Real Friend, 1765
  reprinted 1937.
Fred Miller
  The Training of a Craftsman, 1898.
Clifford Musgrave
  Regency Furniture, 1961. *Adam and Hepplewhite
  and other Neo-Classical Furniture*, 1966.
J. E. Panton
  From Kitchen to Garret, revised edition, 1893.
Hugh Phillips
  Mid-Georgian London, 1964.
E. H. and E. R. Pinto
  Tunbridge and Scottish Souvenir Woodware, 1970.
Passages from the Diaries of Mrs Philip Lybbe Powys,
  ed. Emily J. Climenson, 1899.
Brian Reade
  Regency Antiques, 1953.
Samuel Redgrave
  A Dictionary of Artists of the English School, 2nd
  edition, 1878, reprinted 1970.
  Regency Furniture Designs, ed. John Harris, 1961.
S. von la Roche
  Sophie in London, 1786, trans. Clare Williams, 1933.
H. Clifford Smith
  Buckingham Palace, 1931.
Gladys Scott Thomson
  Family Background, 1949.
John Timbs
  Curiosities of London, 1868.
Horace Walpole
  Letters, ed. Mrs Paget Toynbee, 19 vols., 1903–25.
P. Ward-Jackson
  *English Furniture Designs of the Eighteenth Cen-
  tury*, 1958.
Dora Ware
  A Short Dictionary of British Architects, 1967.
F. J. B. Watson
  Wallace Collection: Catalogues: Furniture, 1956.
  Louis XVI Furniture, 1960.
Geoffrey Wills
  English Looking-Glasses, 1965.

PERIODICALS

Apollo
The Burlington Magazine
The Connoisseur
Country Life

Furniture History
The Gentleman's Magazine
The London Magazine

1 : Thomas Chippendale

IN the minds of many people throughout the world the name of Thomas Chippendale is synonymous with the best mid-18th-Century English mahogany furniture. In spite of his enduring fame, remarkably little is known about the man himself and much of the story of his life and career remains to be discovered. In 1874 Samuel Redgrave published a *Dictionary of Artists of the English School*, in which he recorded:

> Chippendale, Thomas, ornamentist. He was a native of Worcestershire. Came to London, where he first found employment as a joiner, and by his own industry and taste was in the reign of George I. most eminent as a carver and cabinet-maker. . . . No particulars of his life could be ascertained.[1]

Redgrave, who was a painter as well as an efficient civil servant, produced the first book of its kind, and apologised in the Preface for its shortcomings. 'Of an indifferent artist', he wrote, 'information may abound; of one of eminence, concerning whom every fact would be valued, the particulars which exist are meagre in the extreme.' He gave no references for his few facts about the cabinet-maker, and although no great amount has subsequently been discovered about Chippendale almost all Redgrave's statements about him have been refuted.

The principal modern source of details is a book written by Oliver Brackett, of the Department of Woodwork in the Victoria and Albert Museum.[2] In it he reprinted a document, which had first been published in *Notes and Queries* in 1912, dated 1770 and linking Thomas Chippendale, cabinet-maker, of London with a William Chippendale of Otley, Yorkshire. Ten years later, a pedigree appeared in the pages of the same journal, and it was also noted that the registers of the parish church at Otley contained a record of the baptism on 5 June 1718 of 'Thomas Son of John Chippindale of Otley joyner bap yᵉ 5th'.

---

[1] A second, revised, edition was published in 1878, but the entry on Chippendale remained unaltered. This latter edition was reprinted in 1970 (Kingsmead Reprints, Bath).

[2] *Thomas Chippendale, a Study of His Life, Work and Influence*, 1923.

Left, *Plate 1: Cabinet in the 'Chinese Chippendale' style, decorated with Oriental patterns in gold on a black ground and inset with plaques of Italian* pietre dure. *Circa 1760; width 101 cm. (Private collection.)*

Above, *Fig. 1: Advertisement for the* Director *printed in the* General Evening Post *of 31st May 1754.*

The ensuing thirty years are a blank so far as proved facts are concerned, but there are a number of persistent traditions. Some of them are based on remembrances handed down in the family of John Chippendale, Thomas's sixth son, whose descendant, also named John, wrote of them in the pages of *The Cabinet Maker*. According to this report, Thomas Chippendale commenced working with his father at Otley, and 'at an early age his genius became recognised by the Lascelles family, of Harewood House ... later, by the influence of that distinguished family, he, Thomas Chippendale, commenced business in London, where his art appealed to noblemen, and soon his name became famous'.[1]

The future cabinet-maker has also had his name linked with another Yorkshire mansion, Nostell Priory, about 30 miles distant from Otley, where a large doll's house is frequently attributed to him. Nostell was erected between about 1735 and 1750, and the interior was designed by a then unknown young man, James Paine. It has been proposed that the latter met Chippendale in about 1740, and 'Paine suggested to Chippendale that he should go to London in order to study drawing and design ...'.[2]

Paine was born in 1717 and is known to have been a student at the St. Martin's Lane

[1] *The Cabinet Maker*, 31 March 1923. The present Harewood House dates from 1760, but the estate has been in the possession of the Lascelles family since 1739.

[2] Desmond Fitz-Gerald, 'Chippendale's Place in the English Rococo', in *Furniture History*, IV (1968), pages 2–3.

Academy, founded in 1734 by William Hogarth in premises 'large enough to admit thirty or forty people'. The Academy was the training-ground of a number of those who rebelled against the severity of Kent's Palladianism and who duly played an important part in establishing the Rococo in its place.[1] It would seem to be by no means improbable that Thomas Chippendale, if not actually attending the classes was at least acquainted with those who did. They included the French-born engraver Hubert Gravelot, who 'not only designed book illustrations, gold and silversmith's work, but was employed to make drawings for monuments and . . . designed for cabinet-makers, upholsterers, etc.',[2] and was without doubt an important disseminator of the Rococo idiom.

Positive evidence regarding Chippendale's presence in the capital exists in the record of his marriage, which took place on 19th May 1748 at St. George's Chapel, Mayfair, when he was aged about 30. He married Catherine Redshaw, of whom nothing is known beyond the facts that she came from the parish of St. Martin's, bore her husband eleven children and died in 1772. The Chapel was the venue for the clandestine marriages conducted by the notorious Dr. Alexander Keith, whose house in Curzon Street was faced with a Gothic-style doorway to give it a resemblance to a church. Keith made a charge of one guinea for officiating and was finally sent to prison for his activities, but while incarcerated advertised that his curates were deputising for him and no inconvenience would be caused to his clients. His lucrative career terminated when Parliament outlawed his activities, and those of his several confrères, in 1754. Why Chippendale and his bride chose to be wed at the Chapel is not known.

Following the death of his wife, Chippendale remained a widower for five years, and in 1777 married Elizabeth Davis at Fulham parish church. He lived for two years more,

Left, *Fig. 2: Carved mahogany armchair originally in St. Gile's House, Dorset, which was furnished by the Earl of Shaftesbury in the mid-18th Century. The Earl was listed among the subscribers to the* Director *and Chippendale may have made and supplied some of the furniture including this armchair. Circa 1760. (Christie's.)* **Above,** *Fig. 3: Mahogany chair with a carved and pierced back, the legs with carved knees and claw-and-ball feet. This last feature is popularly accepted as a certain sign of Chippendale's influence, but in fact there is not a single piece of furniture with a claw-and-ball foot in any edition of the* Director. *Circa 1750. (Private collection.)*

and was buried on 13th November 1779 at St. Martin's-in-the-Fields, aged 61 or 62.

Of his business career in London from 1749 onwards rather more has been gleaned. By Christmas of that year he was living in Conduit Court, Long Acre; 'as the Court

---

[1] See Mark Girouard, 'Coffee at Slaughter's', 'Hogarth and his Friends' and 'The Two Worlds of St. Martin's Lane', in *Country Life*, 13 January 27 January and 3 February, 1966.

[2] Desmond Fitz-Gerald, op. cit., page 2.

was a mere alley in his day, with an entrance only six feet wide, one wonders how he made furniture of any size in such small premises'.[1] Perhaps the answer to the comment may be that he merely lived there and worked or studied elsewhere. He maintained the tenancy until 1752, and then removed to a house in Northumberland Court, Strand, adjoining Northumberland House.[2]

This Court might also have been described as 'a mere alley', being approached through an arched opening between the eastern wall of the House and a shop kept by a firm of

[1] Hugh Phillips, *Mid-Georgian London*, 1964, page 117.

[2] Sometimes referred to as Somerset Court, ibid., page 119 and Figs. 139 and 142–3.

Below, *Fig. 4: Two-manual harpsichord by Jacob Kirckman. 1755. The walnut case decorated with marquetry and inlay, and the stand supported on carved cabriole legs with claw-and-ball feet. (University of Edinburgh: photograph Sotheby's.)*

Right. *Fig. 5: Carved mahogany armchair of a type popularly labelled 'Chippendale' although none resembling it is to be seen in the pages of the* Director. *Circa 1750. (Phillips, Son and Neale.)*

lace-men. Again, there is no proof that he made furniture on the premises, and he may well have had employment at one of the many cabinet-maker's workshops in the area. Equally, he would have found Northumberland Court, as well as his earlier address, conveniently near the St. Martin's Lane Academy or Slaughter's Coffee House, at the top of the Lane.

Below, Fig. 6: Mahogany basin stand with a tripod base. A jug and basin stood in the ring at the top and when in use the jug rested in the space just above the legs, a round soap ball was kept in the cup provided for it. Circa 1755; height about 76 cm. (Photograph The Connoisseur.)

Right, Fig. 7: Reading or writing table with adjustable top supported on a tripod base with shaped feet. A sturdy functional piece of mahogany furniture that owes nothing to fashionable styling and was possibly made in a provincial workshop. Circa 1755. (Private collection.)

There, students at the Academy met to exchange gossip and ideas, and it was also the resort over the years of many artists from Hogarth to Wilkie.[1]

It was at Christmas 1754 that Chippendale's story begins to assume a more tangible form, when he moved into premises in St. Martin's Lane which he leased for a period of 60 years. Soon afterwards, in April, there was a brief entry in the list of books published which appeared regularly in the *Gentleman's Magazine* (Vol. XXIV, page 195):

> The gentleman's and cabinet-makers director, by *Thomas Chippendale*. 2 l. 8 s.

Thus there was brought to the notice of the public an imposing pattern-book of furniture that established the fame of its author and was the first of its kind to appear in England.

In August 1754 Chippendale acquired a partner, James Rannie, and together they insured the St. Martin's Lane property. The policy was dated 4th February 1755, covered a total sum of £3,700 and was made up as follows:[2]

> . . . the Dwelling House of the said Thomas Chippendale Situate as aforesaid with a warehouse behind adjoining and Communicating on the Right Hand Side of the yard . . . £800
> On their Household Goods utensils and Stock in Trade and Goods in Trust therein and under the said Warehouse and over the roof thereof . . . £1650

---

[1] Following the opening nearby of a rival establishment by the same name, the original Slaughter's, founded in 1692, became known as 'Old Slaughter's'.

[2] The wording of the policy was first reprinted by G. Bernard Hughes, 'Thomas Chippendale's Workshops' in *Country Life*, 14 June 1956, and later by Anthony Coleridge, *Chippendale Furniture*, 1968, page 76.

Glass therein . . .	£100
Wearing apparel in the Dwelling House the property of Thomas Chippendale . . .	£50
. . . a warehouse only intended to be built at the End of the yard . . .	£250
. . . shop only situate On the Left Hand side of the said yard . . .	£150
Utensils Stock in Trade and Goods in Trust Therein . . .	£200
. . . Utensils Stock in Trade and goods in Trust in their Back Yard and in the Shops therein . . .	£500

Two months later, on Saturday 5th April, the *Gentleman's Magazine* recorded (Vol. XXV, page 183):

A Fire broke out at the workshop of Mr Chippendale, a cabinet maker near St Martin's Lane, which consumed the same, wherein were the chests of 22 workmen.

From these various particulars it is plain that within a short time of settling in his new premises Chippendale had acquired a partner and was the employer of at least 22 craftsmen. It suggests that he had achieved considerable success very quickly.

In 1760 Chippendale was elected a member of the Society for the Encouragement of Arts, Manufactures and Commerce, which had been instituted in 1754 to carry out the

Below, *Fig. 8: Chest of drawers decorated with pieces of Chinese incised lacquer, in a manner current, on and off, since the late 17th Century. Circa 1750; width 89 cm. (Christie's.)*

laudable objective of its title; the latter being changed in 1908 to the Royal Society of Arts. He was proposed by a fellow-Yorkshireman, Sir Thomas Robinson, who as an architect had designed his own mansion, Rokeby, and as an extravagant man of fashion and victim of a mania for building ran himself into financial difficulties so that he had to sell his property. At the date of his sponsorship of Chippendale, 'Long Sir Thomas', as he was called, was director of entertainments at the Ranelagh pleasure garden, in London, and was also a member of the committee of the Society arranging an important and successful exhibition of paintings by Reynolds and others.[1] He was an influential figure in the artistic world, and his acquaintance with Chippendale must have been of importance to the latter.

The death of James Rannie occurred in 1766, and in order to settle the estate, the joint stock of furniture and timber was offered for sale. A brief announcement appeared in the *Public Advertiser* during the month of March, and on the 17th was expanded as follows:

***

[1] The idea of such an exhibition, which preceded the formation of the Royal Academy in 1768, was put forward by the artist Francis Hayman, who had studied at the St. Martin's Lane Academy.

Below, *Fig. 9: Mahogany side table, the frieze and legs decorated with fret and with pierced brackets. Circa 1765; width 122 cm. (John Keil, Ltd.)*

TO BE SOLD BY AUCTION

By MR. Pervil

On Monday, the 24th instant, and the following Days. The entire genuine and valuable Stock in Trade of Mr. Chippendale and his late partner Mr. Rennie, deceased, Cabinetmakers and Upholsterers, at their House in St. Martin's Lane, consisting of a great Variety of fine Mahogany and Tulup Wood, Cabinets, Desks, and Book-Cases, Cloaths Presses, double Chests of Drawers, Commodes, Buroes, fine Library, Writing, Card, Dining, and other Tables, Turky and other Carpets, one of which is 13 Feet by 19 Feet six, fine pattern Chairs, and sundry other Pieces of curious Cabinet Work, a large Parcel of fine season'd Feathers; as also all the large unwrought Stock consisting of fine Mahogany and other Woods, in Plank, Boards, Vanier and Wainscot. The whole to be viewed on Friday next to the Hour of Sale (Sunday excepted) which will begin each Day punctually at Twelve.

Catalogues to be had the Days of Viewing at the Place of Sale, and at Mr. Pervil's, the Upper End of Bow-Street, Covent Garden.

The business to be carried on for the future by Mr. Chippendale, on the Premises, on his own Account.

The notice reveals that the firm not only made furniture, but held a stock of feathers for stuffing mattresses, etc., and could supply its clients with carpets of various types. It is also clear from the notice that ready-made articles were kept for buyers who did not demand anything of a special pattern, and it would therefore have been possible to call at the address and select from what was available.

Another partner was admitted in 1771, Thomas Haig, who had been clerk to Rannie. He is assumed to have limited his attention to the counting-house, and to have had little or no direct relation with purely workshop matters.

Chippendale's personal business involvements make some tantalisingly brief appearances in surviving documents. One of them was in January 1768, when he wrote to

Left, Fig. 10: Mahogany fire screen on a tripod base with claw-and-ball feet, the panel of embroidery depicting a basket of flowers. Circa 1750; height overall 150 cm. Chippendale shows designs for three examples of elaborate pattern in the pages of the Director. *(Cotehele House, Cornwall: The National Trust.)*

Below, Fig. 11: Mahogany cabinet with pierced and carved ornament, the door enclosing shelves. Circa 1755; width 91·5 cm. (Mallett and Son, Ltd.)

Sir Rowland Winn, of Nostell, apologising for the delay in completing an order:

> I hope to perform better for the future but it was all owing to the great quantity of unexpected business which I did not Know of nor could refuse doing it as it was mostly for the Royal Family.[1]

In spite of this statement, Chippendale's name does not appear among the names of tradesmen with whom George II or George III did business, nor has it been found in connection with furniture supplied to their families.

In 1771 he was again tardy in making a delivery, this time to Sir Edward Knatchbull, of Mersham-le-Hatch, Kent, and on his behalf Thomas Haig made excuses in a letter dated 23rd November:

> He is extremely sorry that his being detain'd so long in the North, has prevented him waiting on you sooner . . .

The item in dispute, a sheet of glass, was finally sent from London on December 18th, when it was further stated that 'you may expect Mr. Chippendale sometime next week without fail'.[2]

A further fleeting mention records a cross-Channel visit, but while it regrettably gives no reason for the journey an event which was perhaps its sequel is mentioned on page 54. Again writing to Sir Rowland Winn in 1768, this time in October, he blames his foreman's 'inatention to my Buseness' and adds 'I can very safely aver for a truth that I have lost above four Hundred pounds by him upon the whole besides disobliging My Customers'.

> . . . he went into yorkshire and promis'd to be back again in a Very Short time but on the Contrary he stay'd six weeks. He not returning at the time promis'd I left the frame [a case for a barometer] to be going forward till I returned from France.[3]

These extracts are from letters which show that Thomas Chippendale was the active head of a busy firm, and that he was himself concerned with details of the day-to-day affairs. Not only was he engaged in fulfilling his client's requests for both the ordinary and the exotic, but he was continually persuading them to settle their accounts promptly:

> I therefore beg it as the greatest favour that you Will remitt the Money by the return of the post or I shall Certainly be arrested for it and I beg Sʳ Rowland that you will not let that happen to me.[4]

He was not imprisoned, so far as is known, and many of his letters to Sir Rowland Winn and others were in the same heart-breaking vein.

---

[1] Lindsay Boynton and Nicholas Goodison, 'Thomas Chippendale at Nostell Priory', in *Furniture History*, IV (1968), page 25.

[2] Lindsay Boynton, 'Thomas Chippendale at Mersham-le-Hatch', in *Furniture History*, IV (1968), page 87.

[3] Lindsay Boynton and Nicholas Goodison, op. cit., page 26.

[4] Letter of 5 July 1770, ibid., page 27.

Above, *Fig. 12: Carved and gilt 'Confidante' with pierced stretchers.* Circa *1760; width 320 cm. (Stourhead, Wiltshire: The National Trust.)*

Chippendale's death in 1779 at the age of about 62 was attributed in the records to consumption, and it has been suggested that his end was probably due to overwork. There is no evidence, however, in support of the theory and so far as is known he led a normal hard-working businessman's life.

To sum up: remaining documents and letters reveal little more than that Chippendale was a Yorkshireman from Otley who came to London, married twice and had eleven children. Also, he travelled about England and paid at least one visit to France. While other craftsmen and tradesmen of the time occasionally received mentions in memoirs or in gossiping letters, he did not, and his passing went unremarked in the popular papers of the day. His surname is attached internationally to English 18th-Century furniture, and it is a paradox that despite his renown so very little is known about the man himself.

2: The 'Director'

THOMAS Chippendale's book, *The Gentle-man and Cabinet-Maker's Director*, is a folio volume measuring about 46 by 28 cm. (*c*. 18 by 11 inches), and the first edition of it is dated 1754. Although the title-page states that it contains 'one hundred and sixty copper-plates' there are actually 161, because two of them bear the same number, 25. Most of the plates feature more than one piece of furniture, they are dated 1753 and 1754 and were engraved by Matthew Darly and T. and J. S. Müller.

The volume has a dedication to the Earl of Northumberland, owner of the mansion close beside which the author had recently been living. It is short and to the point and in the usual style of such formal addresses:

> My Lord, Your intimate acquaintance with all those Arts & Sciences, that tend to perfect and adorn life, and your well known disposition to promote them give the following Designs a natural claim to your protection, they are therefore with great respect laid at your feet by
> My Lord, Your Lordship's most Humble and obedient Servant
> Thomas Chippendale.

Not only was the Earl a former neighbour, but he was an influential and wealthy man and no doubt these last considerations prompted the dedication. His extravagance was commented upon by Horace Walpole, who wrote to Sir Horace Mann in 1752 commenting on the cost of some copies of paintings purchased by the Earl:

> . . . indeed *price* is no article, or rather *is* a reason for my Lord Northumberland's liking anything. They are building at Northumberland House, at Sion, at Stansted, at Alnwick, and Warkworth Castles! they live by the etiquette of the old peerage, have Swiss porters, the Countess has her pipers—

He concluded the paragraph by forecasting, quite erroneously, 'in short, they will very soon have no estate'.

Next in the book comes the author's Preface. Chippendale opens it by pointing out that cabinet-making owes much to architecture, and that he has 'prefixed to the following Designs a short Explanation of the Five Orders'. After mentioning that 'if no one Drawing should singly answer the Gentleman's taste [the *Gentleman* of the

title], there will yet be found a Variety of Hints, sufficient to construct a new one', he continues

> . . . I frankly confess, that in executing many of the Drawings, my Pencil has but faintly copied out those Images that my Fancy suggested; and had they not been published till I could have pronounced them perfect, perhaps they had never seen the Light.

He closes with these words:

> Upon the whole, I have here given no Design but what may be executed with Advantage by the Hands of a skilful Workman, though some of the Profession have been diligent enough to represent them (especially those after the Gothic and Chinese Manner) as so many specious Drawings, impossible to be worked off by any Mechanic whatsoever. I will not scruple to attribute this to Malice, Ignorance, and Inability; and I am confident I can convince all Noblemen, Gentlemen, or others, who will honour me with their Commands, that every Design in the Book can be improved, both as to Beauty and Enrichment, in the Execution of it, by
> Their Most Obedient Servant,
>   THOMAS CHIPPENDALE.
> St. Martin's Lane,
> Mar. 3., 1754.

The language in which it is couched makes the Preface difficult to interpret;

Left, *Plate 3: Carved mahogany chair made to a design in Chippendale's* Director—*see Fig. 13 (below). Circa 1755; height 99·4 cm. (On loan to Montacute House, Somerset: The National Trust.)*

Below, *Fig. 13: Three 'Ribband Back Chairs' from the* Director, *Plate 16 in the 1754 edition and Plate 15 in that of 1762, engraved by Matthew Darly—compare the right-hand chair with that in Plate 3.*

N° XV.

Ribband Back Chairs.

T. Chippendale inv¹ et del.   *Publish'd according to Act of Parliment*   *M. Darly Sculp.*

THE

GENTLEMAN and CABINET-MAKER's
DIRECTOR:

Being a large COLLECTION of the

Moſt ELEGANT and USEFUL DESIGNS

OF

HOUSEHOLD FURNITURE,

In the Moſt FASHIONABLE TASTE.

Including a great VARIETY of

CHAIRS, SOFAS, BEDS, and COUCHES; CHINA-TABLES, DRESSING-TABLES, SHAVING-TABLES, BASON-STANDS, and TEAKETTLE-STANDS; FRAMES for MARBLE-SLABS, BUREAU-DRESSING-TABLES, and COMMODES; WRITING-TABLES, and LIBRARY-TABLES; LIBRARY-BOOK-CASES, ORGAN-CASES for private Rooms, or Churches, DESKS, and BOOK-CASES; DRESSING and WRITING-TABLES with BOOK-CASES, TOILETS, CABINETS, and CLOATHS-PRESSES; CHINA-CASES, CHINA-SHELVES, and BOOK-SHELVES; CANDLE-STANDS, TERMS for BUSTS, STANDS for CHINA JARS, and PEDESTALS; CISTERNS for WATER, LANTHORNS, and CHANDELIERS; FIRE-SCREENS, BRACKETS, and CLOCK-CASES; PIER-GLASSES, and TABLE-FRAMES; GIRANDOLES, CHIMNEY-PIECES, and PICTURE-FRAMES; STOVE-GRATES, BOARDERS, FRETS, CHINESE-RAILING, and BRASS-WORK, for Furniture.

AND OTHER

ORNAMENTS.

TO WHICH IS PREFIXED,

A Short EXPLANATION of the Five ORDERS of ARCHITECTURE;

WITH

Proper DIRECTIONS for executing the moſt difficult Pieçes, the Mouldings being exhibited at large, and the Dimenſions of each DESIGN ſpecified.

The Whole comprehended in Two HUNDRED COPPER-PLATES, neatly engraved.

Calculated to improve and refine the preſent TASTE, and ſuited to the Fancy and Circumſtances of Perſons in all Degrees of Life.

By THOMAS CHIPPENDALE,

CABINET-MAKER and UPHOLSTERER, in St. Martin's Lane, London.

THE THIRD EDITION.

LONDON:

Printed for the AUTHOR, and ſold at his Houſe, in St. Martin's Lane; Alſo by T. BECKET and P. A. DE HONDT, in the Strand.

MDCCLXII.

what part of it is plain statement of fact and what part a form of words accepted at the time as conventional and now so outdated as to be meaningless or debatable? More than any other, the author's sentence 'my Pencil has but faintly copied out those Images that my Fancy suggested' has been the subject of discussion. This was initiated by the theory that Chippendale himself did not make the original designs, but blatantly put his name to the work of others and claimed falsely that he had been its executant.[1]

THE proposition was that Thomas Chippendale was the 18th Century equivalent of managing director of the business in St. Martin's Lane, and the creative work was done not by him but by men in his employ. Of these, it was said that Matthias Lock[2] was responsible for carved ornament, which doubtless formed the basis for such work depicted in the engravings. On the other hand, Henry Copland prepared all the material for the engraver and made 'sketches for other carver's work commissioned for execution on behalf of clients'. The reasoning behind this concept is admirable for its ingenuity, but more recent thinking has largely dismissed it as untenable on several grounds.

Fiske Kimball and Edna Donnell based their argument mainly on the fact that there is no record of any works published by Lock between his *New Book of Ornaments* of 1752 and his *New Book of Pier-Frame's* of 1769. He must therefore have had some particular employment during those years; years which coincide with the period during most of which Thomas Chippendale was busy preparing his *Director*. More significantly some old albums of drawings in the Victoria and Albert Museum, London, and the Metropolitan Museum, New York, contain unquestioned examples from the hands of both Lock and Chippendale. The presence within the same sets of covers of the work

Left, *Fig. 14: Title-page of the third edition of Chippendale's* Director, *1762.*

Above, *Fig. 15: (Left) Overmantel looking-glass and chimneypiece, and (right) an oval looking-glass, from* A New Book of Ornaments, *by Matthias Lock and Henry Copland, 1752.*

of the two men suggests that they may at least have collaborated, but to what degree is not known. It seems not unlikely that Lock was employed by Chippendale to execute carving, either as a free-lance at an

---

[1] Fiske Kimball and Edna Donnell, 'The Creators of the Chippendale Style', in *Metropolitan Museum Studies*, New York, 1 May 1929.

[2] Geoffrey Wills, *English Furniture 1550–1760*, page 241 et seq.

Above, *Fig. 16: A Chinese scene, from* A New Book of Chinese Designs, *by (George?) Edwards and Matthew Darly, 1754.*

Right, *Fig. 17: Carved mahogany 'French Chair' after the design engraved on Plate 22 in the 1762 edition of the* Director. *The engraving is dated 1759 and the chair was made at about that date.* (Sotheby's.)

address of his own or at St. Martin's Lane, and had no immediate concern with the book.

Henry Copland's share in the publication is even harder to justify. Because he had collaborated with Lock as joint-author of the 1752 *New Book of Ornaments* it was thought likely that he was also involved with him and Chippendale. Nothing is recorded of Copland's activities after that year, it has been remarked that 'for all we know, he may have been dead',[1] but a discovery made subsequent to the writing of those words suggests that he did not die until 1761.[2] An attempt was made to detect his hand in a drawing in the Metropolitan Museum album by judging it against one of his engravings in the *New Book of Ornaments*, but it has been noted that 'comparing the style of an engraving with that of a

drawing must inevitably be an uncertain method of determining authorship'.[3] The drawing cannot therefore be proved to have been made by Copland and none indisputably from his hand have been recorded.

Chippendale included a four-page list of subscribers to the book, numbering in all just over 300 persons with orders for a total of 326 copies. Those named ranged alphabetically from Sir John Anstruther, Bt., of

[1] Peter Ward-Jackson, *English Furniture Designs of the Eighteenth Century*, 1958, page 44.

[2] Geoffrey Wills, op. cit., page 247.

[3] Peter Ward-Jackson, op. cit., page 43.

HOUSHOLD FURNITURE

In Genteel Taste, for the Year 1760.

by a Society of

Upholsterers, Cabinet-Makers, &c.

James McCallum

CONTAINING

Upwards of 180 Designs

on 60 Copper Plates.

Consisting of China, Breakfast, Side-board, Dressing, Toilet, Card, Writing, Clan, Library, Slab, and Night Tables, Chairs, Couches, French Stools, Cabinets, Commodes, China Shelves and Cases, Trays, Chests, Stands for Candles, Tea kettles, Pedestals, Stair-case Lights, Bureaus, Beds, Ornamental Bed-posts, Corniches, Brackets, Fire-Screens, Desk, Book and Clock-cases, Frames for Glasses, Sconce & Chimney-pieces, Girandoles, Lanthorns, Chandalears, &c.a &c.a

with Scales.

Anstruther, Fifeshire, to Messrs. David, John and Robert Young, 'Professors of Philosophy', and included a number of noblemen as well as cabinet-makers, carvers, joiners and upholsterers as well as a surgeon, a bricklayer and two enamellers.

How the subscribers were obtained is at present a mystery. No press advertisements have come to light, and it appears improbable that Chippendale would have known personally even a small proportion of them. Since coming to London he had been occupying quite modest, if central, addresses and had only come to public notice after he opened his St. Martin's Lane establishment some few months prior to the appearance of the *Director*. Possibly he followed the precedent of Samuel Johnson, whose Dictionary was issued in 1755, and who had previously written and issued a prospectus addressed to the Earl of Chesterfield: entitled *A Plan for a Dictionary of the English Language*. This was printed and circulated in 1747, so there was an eight-year gap between the *Plan* and its fruition. Chippendale's task was a less arduous one than Johnson's and he would probably have required less time in which to complete it, but this is no more than conjecture. Perhaps a printed prospectus for the *Director* will be discovered one day, as there seems to be no other method by which the author could have gathered such a number of purchasers from all parts of England and Scotland. There was a noticeably high proportion from the latter country, and it may be wondered by what means they were induced to buy the volume.

Between the list of subscribers and the plates themselves is a commentary on the latter, which lists brief remarks on the articles depicted and occasionally strays from the strictly factual. Thus, with reference to the chairs in Fig. 13, he remarked that they were 'the best I have ever seen (or perhaps have ever been made)', while of a china case he wrote that it was 'not only the richest and most magnificent in the whole [sic], but perhaps in all Europe'—possibly his enthusiasm having caused him to overlook omission of the words 'of England'.

The plates were the work of more than one engraver; the majority of them bearing the name of Matthew Darly, who became tenant of Chippendale's house in Northumberland Court when the latter moved to St. Martin's Lane. Darly had published his own *New Book of Chinese, Gothic and*

Left, *Fig. 18: Engraved title-page of* Houshold Furniture ... *for the Year 1760, containing designs by Thomas Chippendale and others.* **Below,** *Fig. 19: Pier-glasses, signed design by Thomas Chippendale for Plate 173 in the third edition of the* Director, *1762. Drawing in pen and ink and wash; 33·6 × 18 cm. (Victoria and Albert Museum.)*

Above, *Fig. 20: Mahogany tea table, the carved and pierced tray top raised on a carved tripod base with scroll feet. Circa 1760; height 73·7 cm. No designs for tables of this variety are in the* Director, *but some are in* Houshold Furniture *(see page 32). (Christie's.)*

Right, *Fig. 21: Pair of parcel-gilt mahogany candle stands with galleried tops and tripod bases. Circa 1760; height 111·7 cm. Several of more complicated patterns appear in the* Director. *(Christie's.)*

Modern Chairs, with plates dated 1751 and 1752, and in 1754 collaborated in *A New Book of Chinese Designs* (Fig. 16). The engravings in this are signed by Edwards and Darly, and it has been proposed[1] that the latter was George Edwards, well-known as a naturalist who wrote and illustrated *The Natural History of Uncommon Birds* and *Gleanings of Natural History*, which were published between 1743 and 1764. Those plates in the *Director* not engraved by Darly were the work of Tobias and Johann Sebastian Müller, who were born in

Nuremburg, settled in London and duly changed their surname to Miller.

The 1754 edition of the *Director* was followed by a second in 1755, which is virtually a duplicate of the earlier one. While the book might have sold so well on its first appearance as to demand a quick reprinting, it is possible that there was another reason for issuing a further edition. The late Alex G. Lewis put forward the idea that this may have been the fire in the workshops on 5 April 1755 (see page 10), which could well have destroyed the author's own stock of copies.[2]

SEVEN years later, in 1762, a third edition was published. Of the 161 plates in the first, 95 were retained and 105 new ones added to make a total of 200. Most of the fresh engravings show articles more elaborate in pattern than before, and some pieces of furniture that had been omitted previously were included, such as washstands, shaving-tables, cisterns and pedestals, hall chairs and garden seats. Looking-glass frames and girandoles were almost all replaced by new patterns. The dedication to the Earl of Northumberland is usually found to have been retained, but a few copies have been recorded which contain a dedication to Prince William Henry. He was a younger brother of George III, grandson of Frederick Louis, Prince of Wales, and was created Duke of Gloucester

---

[1] Martin Hardie, *Water-colour Painting in Britain*, 3 vols., 1966–8, vol. I, page 68.

[2] Anthony Coleridge, *Chippendale Furniture*, 1968, page 89.

in 1764. The wording of the scarcer dedication reads in part:

> . . . May it please your Royal Highness, to take the following Work under Your Protection, Your Royal Highness's Ready Condescension to encourage whatever is Laudable and useful. . . . emboldens the Author to lay it at your Royal Highness's Feet. . . .

It may be thought the phrasing implies that Chippendale, presumptuously, had not requested permission from the Prince before he printed the page, and that it was withdrawn from circulation as a result of a complaint to that effect.

The preliminary pages of the third edition were revised, and the number of engravers employed on the plates increased. They now comprised, in addition to Darly and the Müllers, Butler Clowes, Isaac Taylor, James Hulett, W. Foster, C. H. Hemerick (who was, like the Müllers, from Nuremburg), (?T.) Morris and Edward Rooker. A few of the plates bore only the name of Chippendale as designer and lacked that of an engraver.

Below, *Fig. 22: Carved mahogany commode after a design in the first edition of* the Director *and attributed to Chippendale's workshop.* Circa 1755; width 127 cm. (Søtheby's.)

Right, *Fig. 23: Mahogany hanging bookshelves, the pierced pattern including Gothic cusps and other motifs.* Circa 1765; width about 70 cm. (Mallet and Son, Ltd.)

All or most of the above men would seem to have been students at the St. Martin's Lane Academy, or to have been connected with someone who had attended there. This is perhaps not surprising in view of the fact that it was the sole establishment of its type in London at the time, and was only supplanted after the founding of the Royal Academy schools in 1768. In addition, the area was a favourite one with artists and craftsmen of all kinds, especially cabinet-makers, and doubtless in the London of the 1750's each and every one of them was acquainted.

The third edition was also issued with a title-page and description of the plates in French 'for the Convenience of Foreigners'. There is, however, no record of the impact made across the Channel by

> *Le Guide du Tapissier, de l'Ebéniste et de tous ceux qui travaillent en meubles . . .*

and the publication may well have made more of an impression in London. There, it would have suggested a business of international importance, while in France the *ébénistes* would take good care that anyone from outside their highly-organised

Below, *Fig. 24: Mahogany 'Tea Chest' for holding silver caddies, resembling a* Director *design. Circa 1760; width 25·5 cm. (Private collection.)*

Right, *Plate 4: Mahogany chest fitted with a secretaire, the fall front simulating two long drawers. Circa 1760; width 77 cm. (Private collection.)*

ranks made little or no headway.

A further edition of the *Director*, the fourth, was probably planned, and some of Chippendale's drawings for it are in the Metropolitan Museum. Versions of the drawings are in the Victoria and Albert Museum. There survive also some of the drawings he made for another book, *Houshold Furniture In Genteel Taste for the Year 1760*, in which were contributions by 'a Society of Upholsterers, Cabinet-Makers, etc.' (Fig. 18). The first edition of the book contains 60 engraved plates depicting about 180 articles, of which nos. 6, 48, 49 and 51 are signed 'Couse sculp'. Redgrave mentions him in a few short sentences:

> Couse, J., engraver. Supposed born in England. Practised here about 1750. His works are little known. Strutt says some views which he engraved prove him to have been no indifferent artist.[1]

There is no information about the 'Society of Upholsterers', but the members in addition to Chippendale, have been identified as Robert Manwaring, William Ince and John Mayhew and Thomas Johnson.[2] The volume was issued by one of the most enterprising publishers of the day, Robert Sayer of Fleet Street. The various cabinet-makers concerned may not have formed a society in the accepted sense, and their

corporate title may have been brought into existence, perhaps by Sayer, to provide an authoritative-sounding line on the title-page of the book.

A second edition of *Houshold Furniture* was expanded considerably so that it shows some 350 articles on 120 plates, and the date was omitted from the title. A copy of it, divided into four parts of which each has a separate title-page, is in the Victoria and Albert Museum. Yet another edition has the title *Household Furniture for the Year 1763*. Had Chippendale's own drawings for this unpretentious work not survived it is doubtful that anyone would have considered connecting his name with it. The various editions depict mostly commonplace pieces of no great distinction, and the draughtmanship is only of average standard. It is very different in every way from the *Director*, which remains unequalled after two centuries.

---

[1] Samuel Redgrave, op. cit. E. Bénézit, *Dictionnaire . . .*, 8 vols., 1960, adds that Couse engraved a *View of Berkeley Castle* after a drawing by the Countess of Berkeley, and confuses the reader with a glaring misprint by stating that he worked in England '*vers 1570*'.

[2] Peter Ward-Jackson, op. cit., pages 51–2.

3 : 'French', 'Chinese', and 'Gothic'

CHIPPENDALE's *Director* was what would be termed today a prestige publication, primarily demonstrating the variety of articles his firm could make and supply. It had a secondary purpose in informing his fellow cabinet-makers who wanted to keep their designs up to date. Subsequently, the book has provided an important guide to what was current at the dates of issue, has continued to stimulate research into 18th Century furniture and has kept alive its author's name.

The engravings in the two principal editions of the book, the first of 1754 and the third of 1762, differ more in the variety of goods they depict than in the styles in which they appear. In 1754 there were twelve plates showing 38 chairs, while eight years later 60 chairs were on 21 plates. Perversely, the one feature that many people couple with the name of Chippendale, the claw-and-ball foot, is absent from the book. Although there was duplication of some of the designs there was a wide range from which to select, and in the words of Anthony Coleridge 'it is therefore not surprising that many chairs stemming from these designs have survived'.[1]

The designs throughout can mostly be divided into three categories: French, Chinese and Gothic. It will be found, however, that the division is a very loose one with considerable overlapping, so that in some instances it is difficult to determine which of the three styles is paramount. Alternatively, there are a number of updated versions of earlier Palladian pieces, which result in what may be termed conveniently light-weight Kent. In this manner is the gilt side table in Plate 5, which can claim kinship to a 'Sideboard Table' on Plate LXI of the 1762 edition. The Rococo central feature and ornament on the frieze and legs contrast with the simple lines of the whole, and apart from the carving the piece might be described as 'ageless'.

Typical of Chippendale's version of the French style is the armchair illustrated in Fig. 17, for which a design in the *Director* of 1762 is on Plate XXII, engraved by Isaac Taylor and dated 1759. Its equivalent made

---

[1] Anthony Coleridge, op. cit., page 95.

in France would have been carved in walnut or beech-wood and gilt or painted, but it is here executed in mahogany. The lavish use of Rococo 'C'-scrolls, floral sprays and general assymetry reached the peak of popularity in the decade 1750–60, and these features are arrayed in chairs of this type so that the fluid and graceful lines tend to disguise the essential strength of the article.

The 1762 *Director* contains designs for formal hall chairs, with plain wood seats and in some instances incorporating an owner's coat of arms or monogram and coronet in the back. There is also a page of garden furniture, two armchairs and a settee, appropriately rustic in appearance and designated for use in arbours or summer-houses, grottoes or at the end of long walks. While two of them make use of large shell-shapes in the backs, an armchair also has one flattened to form a seat and like the other offers little prospect of comfort as seen on the printed page. The second of the chairs has an oval back composed of leaves centred on a trophy of gardening implements. As the century progressed there were a number of makers who specialised in furniture of this type, such as William

Left, *Plate 5: Giltwood table carved with floral and other motifs popularised by Chippendale, the top of veneered marble. Circa 1760; width 155 cm. (John Keil, Ltd.)*

Below, *Fig. 25: Carved mahogany commode based on a design in the* Director. *Circa 1755; width 139·7 cm. (Christie's.)*

Above, *Fig. 26: One of a number of designs for Chinese-style cabinets in the* Director; *this engraving is dated 1753 but others were executed in 1760 and 1761.* Opposite, *Fig. 27: Parcel-gilt mahogany display cabinet in the Chinese style, the centre drawer in the stand fitted for writing, based on designs in the* Director—*see Fig. 26. Circa 1755; width 157·5 cm. (Pelham Galleries Ltd.)*

Webb who stated that he was a

> Maker of Yew Tree, Gothic and Windsor chairs, China and Rural Seats. . .[1]

Often exposed to the elements, the majority of garden furniture has perished long ago, and its existence is known only from pattern-books, trade-cards and bills.

Chippendale's book continues with pieces for a variety of purposes, as detailed on the title-page (Fig. 14). Those claiming a Chinese ancestry are distinguished by a use of fretted ornament, to which two pages at the end of the volume are devoted. Although entitled 'Chinese Railing' and depicting the fret supported by posts, it is of similar design to that visible on the pieces of furniture elsewhere in the volume.

The Oriental-style designs shown are little more than caricatures of the real thing, but as few English people had then travelled much farther eastwards than Rome, this was not important. While earlier nothing less than the genuine imported article, or a close substitute, had proved satisfactory, the mid-18th Century public was content with an obvious and light-hearted imitation. The architect, Sir William Chambers, who paid a visit to Canton in 1748–9, did his best to persuade his countrymen of their error in innocently accepting such travesties as authentic. He published a book entitled *Designs of Chinese Buildings, Furniture, Dresses, Machines and Utensils* in 1757, and wrote in it that he hoped they 'might be of use in putting a stop to the extravagances that daily appear under the name of Chinese'.

One of Chambers own efforts to enlighten the ignorant is the Pagoda, still standing in Kew Gardens, Surrey, which he designed for the Princess Dowager of Wales, widow of Frederick Louis, in 1761. His earnestness and attention to what he considered absolute accuracy did not, however, endear his versions of Chinese art to his patrons, who continued to prefer the misrepresentations he criticised. Sir William lost his battle with the lovers of untruth, and left a more popular and less controversial monument in the form of Somerset House, in the Strand.

In addition to zig-zag frets of various patterns, Chippendale and his contemporaries made much use of the fluted pagoda roof, which they adapted to the tops of cabinets and the backs of chairs (Fig. 27). While the Chinese themselves added flatly-drawn flowers as a surface decoration to porcelain, wall-papers and much else, the English cabinet-makers carved similar ornament in

---

[1] Ambrose Heal, *London Furniture Makers*, 1953, page 197.

Fig. 28: *Right-hand portion of Plate 181 in the third edition of Chippendale's* Director, *engraved by Butler Clowes and dated 1761.*

high relief. Thus, the finished article would be given its quota of Oriental touches, but was thoroughly anglicised by the addition of a profusion of floral sprays and the inevitable, completely Western, 'C'-scrolls.

Contrasting with the delicacy and elaboration of the East, was the simplicity and solidity of Gothic. That the taste for it at the time was less widespread than for French and Chinese may be deduced from the fact that Chippendale included only a single plate of 'Gothick frets' for the guidance of readers. On the other hand, there was no lack of designs for pieces in the style, all of which embodied lancet-shaped panels, mouldings or glazing-bars, and were decorated with cusps and suitable tracery.

BY the mid-century, fashionable taste turned firmly to France for its inspiration, but the country and subjects ruled by Louis XV lost their appeal for many of their admirers when the monarch joined with Austria against England and her ally Prussia in the Seven Years War of 1756–63. The political reaction had appeared earlier in one form as the Anti-Gallican Society; founded in 1745, it was intended 'to oppose the insidious arts of the French nation'. More explicitly,

> . . . from the Endeavours of its members to promote British manufactures, to extend the commerce of England and discourage the introduction of French modes and oppose the importation of French commodities.

The Society is perhaps best remembered by collectors of antiques, because the badge bearing its arms, and the motto 'For Our Country', was made in English enamel. It also penetrated the world of ceramics, for the arms are found on Chinese porcelain punch-bowls decorated to the order of

English enthusiasts. Otherwise, the Society does not seem to have caused much of a stir, and limited itself to awarding small money prizes to what it considered anti-French actions; such as making lace to compete successfully with the imported (or smuggled) product.

The apparently weak impact of the Anti-Gallican Society reflected the spirit of the time, for, while the French were undoubtedly the arch-enemy, their civilisation held a magic attraction. Even if it was considered by the few to be unpatriotic, the majority of English people salved their conscience by looking on Art as international. A few of them, however, defiantly adopted what they considered to be a truly English style of decoration, one which owed nothing to devious foreigners but was a wholesome native product.

The chosen style was Gothic, which had been largely confined to the decoration of church exteriors and interiors since medieval times. From the early 18th Century it had begun to be revived for domestic architecture, and both Sir John Vanburgh and William Kent added battlements and similar features to some of their buildings. In 1742 Batty Langley, who published books on numerous styles, published one with the title *Gothic Architecture Restored and Improved*, which indicates that the subject was gaining interest.

The leading Gothicist of the mid-century was Horace Walpole, fourth son of the eminent statesman, Sir Robert Walpole. The former was also a member of Parliament for about thirty years, but is best remembered today for his letters, which have been printed. He lived from 1717 to 1797, so his life spanned the major part of the century of which much is revealed in the careful phraseology and wit of his writing.

It was in May 1747 that Walpole purchased the remainder of the lease of a house near Twickenham, then known as Strawberry Hill-Shot. He took it over from Mrs. Chenevix, proprietress of a well-known shop

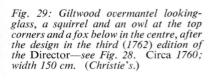
Fig. 29: Giltwood overmantel looking-glass, a squirrel and an owl at the top corners and a fox below in the centre, after the design in the third (1762) edition of the Director—*see Fig. 28. Circa 1760; width 150 cm. (Christie's.)*

at Charing Cross, whose stock-in-trade was similar to that of her father, William Deards. He was in business nearby, at Craven Street, Strand, with a branch at Bath, and his card announced that he 'buys and sells Jewells, Gold and Silver Plate, Fine Toys, &c.'.[1] Toys, in fact, for grown-ups.

On 5 June 1747 Walpole noted in a letter written in London to his friend, Sir Horace Mann, in Florence:

> This little rural *bijou* was Mrs Chenevix's, the toy-woman *à la mode*, who in every dry season is to furnish me with the best rain-water from Paris, and now and then with some Dresden china cows, who are to figure like wooden classics in a library. . . .[2]

Two years later he had purchased the property outright, and in January 1750 stated:

> I am going to build a little Gothic castle at Strawberry Hill.[3]

By 1753 the proposed alterations were effected and he was able to relate what he had achieved. As regards the entrance, he

---

[1] Hugh Phillips, *Mid-Georgian London*, 1964, pages 94, 123 and 125.

[2] *Letters of Horace Walpole*, ed. Toynbee, 19 vols., Oxford, 1903–25, vol. ii, page 278.

[3] Ibid., vol. ii, page 423.

Fig. 30: Carved mahogany writing table, at one time at Coombe Abbey, Warwickshire; the house is thought to have been supplied with furniture made by Chippendale. Circa 1760; width 244 cm. (Sotheby's.)

wrote:

> . . . under two gloomy arches, you come to the hall and staircase, which it is impossible to describe to you, as it is the most particular and chief beauty of the castle. Imagine the walls covered with (I call it paper, but it is really paper painted in perspective to represent) Gothic fretwork: the lightest Gothic balustrade to the staircase, adorned with antelopes (our supporters) bearing shields; lean windows fattened with rich saints in painted glass, and a vestibule open with three arches on the landing-place, and niches full of trophies of old coats of mail, Indian shields made of rhinoceros hides, broadswords, quivers, long bows, arrows, and spears. . . .[1]

In due course the owner added a number of rooms and a tower to his property, and was able to convert a few of his many friends to his liking for what he termed 'monastic gloomth'.

Fully authenticated Chippendale furniture is extremely rare, and the principal collections still remaining in the houses for which they were originally supplied are at Nostell Priory and Harewood House, both in Yorkshire. A somewhat larger number of mansions retain only a few examples, and others are known to have been supplied by the firm with furniture which is unfortunately no longer identifiable. A further few,

---

[1] Ibid., vol. iii, page 166.

Fig. 31: 'Library Table' engraved by Tobias Müller in 1753; the engraving is Plate 57 in the first edition of the Director *and Plate 83 in the third. The table in Fig. 30 (opposite) closely corresponds to this design in some respects.*

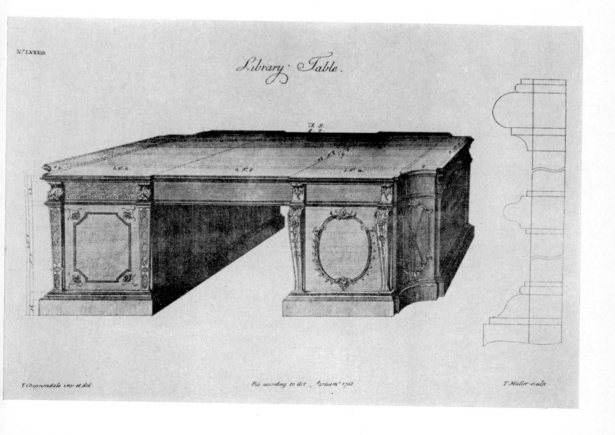

Library Table.

N.º LXXXIII

T. Chippendale inv. et del.   Pub. according to Act. Parliam.t 1753   T. Müller sculp.

Fig. 32, page 42: Mahogany writing table of Gothic design; the cluster-columns and the 'church-window' mouldings are typical of the style. Circa 1760; width 183 cm. (Private collection.) Fig. 33, page 43: Settee and armchair from a suite of giltwood furniture at Saltram, Devon. They resemble pieces supplied to Harewood House, Yorkshire, by Thomas Chippendale, and as records of payments to Chippendale by John Parker of Saltram survive it is most probable that the suite was made at the St. Martin's Lane workshops. Circa 1770; width of settee 254 cm. (Saltram, Devon: The National Trust.) **Right,** *Fig. 34: Mahogany bookcase showing a delicate and elaborate employment of Gothic features. Circa 1765; width about 122 cm. (Mallett and Son, Ltd.)*

the majority in point of numbers, are represented by bills and letters which have been preserved but can no longer be related to the articles they detail.[1]

Although the dispersal of so much of this furniture is to be regretted, the surviving documents provide a considerable amount of information. From them it is to be learned that Chippendale's firm supplied not only furniture for the grand apartments of noblemen's mansions, but attended to such commonplace tasks as paper-hanging, curtain-making and the hundred and one jobs carried out by the complete interior decorator.

At Mersham-le-Hatch in 1767 he charged Sir Edward Knatchbull for the following, among numerous other items of the same variety:

Papering &c.		
To Paste & Hanging the Alcove Bedchamber	1.	3. 0.
12 Pieces of Strip'd Verditure[2]	4.	16. 0.
6 doz. Borders		12. 0.
Paste & Hanging the Closet Adjoining with 2 Papers		10. 0.
2 Papers for ditto		4. 6.
Verditure and Colouring the Room	1.	1. 0.

Elsewhere in the house he charged for:

Thread tape & Making up & fixing 3 Old Crimson Cheque Window Curtains in Sir Edward's Room		13. 6.
2 12/4 fine Blankets	3.	3. 0.
An under Blanket		12. 0.
To 3 Carpet Brooms & 2 Jappan'd Hearth Brooms		12. 0.[3]

Comparable work was carried out at Harewood House, where the more costly pieces of furniture, as elsewhere, were supplied with cloth covers to preserve them from dust and damage when they were not in use, and the damask-hung walls were similarly protected with specially-made 'Canvass and paper Hangings'. Of the famed library table, once in the house and now at Temple Newsam, there is no record in the existing portion of Chippendale's accounts, but there is a note to the effect that one of his employees, named Reid, was 'Making covers for the Library Table and stool' in April 1772.[4]

---

[1] All are listed by Anthony Coleridge, op. cit., pages 105–23.

[2] Verditure: Johnson describes this as 'The faintest and palest green'.

---

[3] See Lindsay Boynton, 'Thomas Chippendale at Mersham-le-Hatch', in *Furniture History*, IV (1968), pages 81–104. Some of the furniture formerly in the house is discussed and illustrated by Peter Thornton, 'The Furnishing of Mersham-le-Hatch', in *Apollo*, April and June 1970.

[4] Anthea Stephenson, 'Chippendale Furniture at Harewood', in *Furniture History*, IV (1968), pages 62–80. The design of the table was for a long time attributed to Robert Adam, but now both design and manufacture are firmly accepted as being by Chippendale.

The workshops in St. Martin's Lane, at the sign of *The Chair*, must have been busily employed, and no doubt by the 1770's the staff had increased from the 22 known to have been employed there in 1755 (see page 10). On the other hand, Chippendale would have followed the usage of his day, and the present, by contracting-out a proportion of the work to specialists. The carving and gilding of looking-glass and picture frames, for instance, was only very rarely executed under the same roof as straightforward furniture-carving. Likewise, while he may have held a stock of plate glass on the premises, it is improbable that he would have had facilities for bevelling the edges if required, and would have sent it out to a grinder. The same practice would no doubt have been followed as regards polishing and silvering.

Right, *Plate 6: Looking-glass in a carved giltwood frame, closely resembling another in the Victoria and Albert Museum which has been attributed to Chippendale. Circa 1765; height about 183 cm. Beneath is a two-door satinwood commode painted* en grisaille. *Circa 1785; width 137 cm. (Private collection.)*

Fig. 36, page 48: Mahogany secretaire-cabinet supplied to Paxton House, Berwickshire, in 1774 and invoiced by Chippendale, Haig & Co. as 'A large mahogany Chiffonier Table off very fine wood with a drawer with Ink and Sand Bottles and a Slider covered with Cloath . . . £3. 8. 0.' Width 124·5 cm. (Christie's.)

Fig. 35: Writing-table inlaid with various woods on a rosewood ground, formerly at Harewood House, Yorkshire, and almost certainly made by Thomas Chippendale. Circa 1770; width 206 cm. (Temple Newsam House, Yorkshire: Leeds City Art Gallery.)

4 : Chippendale's Contemporaries

Left, *Plate 7: Mahogany serpentine-fronted chest of four long drawers and a baize-lined brushing slide, the angles carved in a Rococo pattern and the whole raised on pierced bracket feet. Circa 1760; width 110 cm. Swing-frame dressing mirror on bow-fronted box base; c. 1785, width 46·5 cm. (Private collection.)*

Right, *Fig. 38: Mahogany cupboard, the doors with simulated part-drawers and carved with swags of flowers, the oval mouldings on the front and sides characteristic of documented pieces by William Vile, to whom this piece is attributed. Circa 1760; width 127 cm. (Metropolitan Museum of Art, New York: photograph Christie's.)*

THOMAS Chippendale's pre-eminence as an 18th-Century cabinet-maker rests on the evidence of his book and on the surviving examples of the furniture he supplied. However, some of his contemporaries made pieces that were not inferior to his, although they did not go so far as to publicise their designs, or themselves, in the way that Chippendale did.

Foremost among them was the firm of Vile and Cobb, also with premises in St. Martin's Lane, a matter of a few doors away from 'The Chair', where they established themselves in 1750. Documented examples of furniture they supplied are of outstandingly high quality as regards both design and execution, but it is not uncommon for pieces to be attributed to them on slender grounds. It has been pointed out that Vile and Cobb possibly employed one or more designers who, like carvers, may well have worked at more than one establishment taking their personal quirks of style from one to another.[1]

In the early 1760's William Vile was working for members of the Royal family, and some of his documented pieces remain at Buckingham Palace and Windsor Castle. He also supplied furniture to Lord Folkestone at Longford Castle, Wiltshire, which is still there and for which his high charges were criticised at the time.

To Vile's earlier days are attributed some of a recorded series of heavily-carved writing-tables of distinctive design (see *English Furniture 1550–1760*, pages 234–6). Later, he made successful use of the Rococo style, often with the noticeable feature of an applied carved oval moulding on the fronts of pieces. It is an idiosyncrasy which was doubtless not exclusive to any one workshop, but is accepted by some modern writers as being in the nature of a trademark. The oval is seen on the doors and sides of the cupboard in Fig. 38, where it is allied with carefully-chosen veneers and impeccable workmanship.

---

[1] See Ralph Edwards, 'Attributions to William Vile', in *Country Life*, 7 October 1954.

William Vile retired from business in 1765, after which John Cobb traded on his own but did not succeed his former partner as Cabinet-Maker to the Royal Household. Such as it is, rather more information is available about Cobb himself than about most other cabinet-makers. His marriage was reported in a newspaper of 1755, and his alliance with a family already well-established in the furniture trade must have proved of assistance to him in his own business. The announcement reads:

> The same Day [Monday 31 May] was married at St. John's, Clerkenwell, Mr. John Cobb, Partner with Mr. Vile, the Corner of Long-Acre, to Miss Sukey Grendey, Daughter of Mr. Grendey, an eminent Timber Merchant in St. John's Square.[1]

[1] *General Evening Post*, 1 April 1755 (No. 3519). For Giles Grendey see *English Furniture 1550–1760*, pages 130, 188, 231 and 235.

John Thomas Smith, who was for some years Keeper of Prints and Drawings at the British Museum, wrote a two-volume book of reminiscences full of period gossip. In it he recorded:

> The corner house of Long-Acre, now No. 72, formed a small part of the extensive premises formerly occupied by that singularly haughty character, Cobb, the Upholsterer . . . [He] was perhaps one of the proudest men in England; and always appeared in full

Below, *Fig. 39: Rosewood three-drawer commode with gilt metal handles, corner and foot mounts in the French manner, perhaps by John Cobb. Circa 1765; width 120·6 cm. (Christie's.)* **Right,** *Fig. 40: Mahogany chest of drawers fitted with a secretaire and bookshelves, the latter with back and sides of Chinese-style fret. Circa 1760; width 63·5 cm. (Sotheby's.)*

Left, *Fig. 41: Stand for a tea urn, the slide supporting a tea pot for refilling with hot water, made of mahogany and with moulded cabriole legs terminating in scroll toes.* Circa 1765; height 56 cm. (*Christie's.*) **Right**, *Fig. 42: Mahogany stand, the top with a turned gallery and carved apron and the moulded scroll legs united by a pierced stretcher.* Circa 1760; height 63·5 cm. (*Temple Newsam House, Yorkshire: Leeds City Art Gallery.*)

dress of the most superb and costly kind, in which state he would strut through his workshops, giving orders to his men.[1]

Smith noted that Cobb 'occasionally employed Banks, the Cellaret-maker, to whom I applied for information respecting him'. Benjamin Banks had his place of business in Litchfield Street, Soho, and was practitioner of a specialised branch of cabinet-making which was concerned with boxes and cases of various descriptions.

Cobb has for long been known to have made an 'extra neat inlaid commode' delivered to Paul Methuen at Corsham Court, Wiltshire, in 1772. A similar one is illustrated in Fig. 37, from which it can be seen that the description is no exaggeration as both design and workmanship are of a high

standard. The piece is in the French style, but unlike earlier ones on the same model, e.g. Figs. 22 and 25, it is ornamented with marquetry instead of with carving. In the authentic French manner, mounts of cast gilt metal set off the woodwork and protect the vulnerable angles and feet.

Not all such pieces were inlaid, and a proportion relied on their lines and the grain of their veneers to achieve the required effect. The example in Fig. 39 has a feature seldom seen in English cabinet-making, in which no attempt is usually made to conceal the transverse members between drawers. Here, however, the French practice has been followed, and the lowest drawer has a shaped apron to hide the cross-piece.

John Cobb died in 1778, leaving half his fortune to his wife Mary, from which it may be assumed that he re-married, and administration of his will was granted on the affidavit of William Hallet and John Graham. Hallet (whose name is sometimes spelt Hallett) had premises next door to those of Cobb. He is known to have made

[1] J. T. Smith, *Nollekens and His Times*, second edition, 2 vols., 1829; Smith worked as a youth in the studio of the sculptor, Joseph Nollekens, and wrote of the latter in the first volume of his book, the second is filled with anecdotes of his contemporaries.

Left, *Fig. 43: Mahogany chair with a carved and pierced back, the cluster-column legs united by pierced stretchers. Circa 1760; height 99 cm. (Temple Newsam House, Yorkshire: Leeds City Art Gallery.)* **Right,** *Fig. 44: Mahogany night commode, the detachable upper part forming a bed-table. Circa 1760; width about 55 cm. (Henry Rubin Esq.)*

furniture for a number of important clients, but the only piece as yet positively identified as having come from his workshop is a mahogany cabinet of Palladian design.[1] On sight it would be dated to c. 1740, but a minute examination of the interior of the carcase revealed the pencilled inscription 'William Hallet 1763 Long Acre'.

Hallet's career included the purchase in 1747 of a portion of the Cannons estate, near Edgware, Middlesex, on which the Duke of Chandos had built a great mansion. It had been completed for only a score of years when financial difficulties and the death of the owner led to its sale and demolition.

Vile and Cobb and Hallet were neighbours at the top end of St. Martin's Lane and were obviously on such close terms that they co-operated in legal matters: Hallet was a trustee in 1763 of William Vile's will as well as being concerned with that of

---

[1] Illustrated by Anthony Coleridge, op. cit., plates 69–71.

Cobb. It has been suggested that they were perhaps also partners in business, and it is not unlikely that the adjoining firms would have had at least an informal trading agreement. A large order would possibly have been beyond the resources of either one of them alone, so what more natural than to share it with the man next door?

John Cobb's employment of the Louis XV style for his identified work was doubtless to suit the taste of his clients, but his own knowledge of it certainly sprang from contact with examples of French manufacture. In 1772, complaints from some London cabinet-makers reached the ears of Parliament, and Customs officials learned 'that a very large Quantity of Foreign Work was for Sale in the Houses of Messieurs Wall and Riley, in Sherrard [Gerrard] Street, Mr. Cullen, in Greek Street, and Mr. Cobbs, in Saint Martin's Lane'. The officers visited each of the places in turn, and seized large amounts of contraband goods. From John Cobb's, where the haul was the smallest in size but possibly the highest in

value, they took the following:

A Writing Table.
One D°, with a Cabinet on its Top.
A Commode, with a Marble Slab.
A Coin, with a Marble Slab.
One Ditto, with a Ditto.
A Commode with a Marble Slab.
One Ditto with a Ditto.
A Writing Table.
A Coin, with a Marble Slab.
One Ditto, with a Ditto.
A Writing Table.
4 Architrave Glass Frames, in Pieces, gilt.
11 Keys belonging to the above Commodes, &c.[1]

The report on the affair refers briefly to the goods listed, 'which the Officers alledge they can prove were then to be sold; and that they saw the Goods in March last, with a much greater Quantity, and the Prices affixed thereon, amounting to upwards of £3,000'.

It was found that all the furniture had been imported duty-free in the diplomatic bags of the Neapolitan and Venetian representatives, and that they had been deposited at the three places allegedly on a 'sale or return' basis. This last is doubtful, as there is clear evidence that both Walle and Reilly and James Cullen were later concerned in other smuggling ventures of the same nature. It is probable

---

[1] A 'Writing Table, with a Cabinet on its Top' would have been a flat-topped table with its matching file for documents (a *bureau-plat* and *cartonnier*). A 'Coin' was the anglicised term for a corner-cabinet (*encoignure*).

Opposite, *Fig. 45: Master's armchair of mahogany, the back pierced in a Gothic pattern and the front legs partly squared and partly tapering. Circa 1760; height about 150 cm. (Private collection.)*
Below, *Fig. 46: Mahogany writing table with serpentine front, back and sides, the angles carved with Rococo ornament. Circa 1760; width about 244 cm. (Mallett and Son, Ltd.)*

Fig. 47: Mahogany bookcase with cupboard below, the cornice decorated with a band of 'blind' fret and surmounted by pierced and moulded swans' necks. Circa 1765; width about 137 cm. (Mallett and Son, Ltd.)

that the three of them, as well as Cobb, were merely making use of the complaisant diplomats and possibly rewarding them for their trouble.[1]

In the 20th Century the buying and selling of duty-free articles plays only a very minor part in daily life, and no part at all in the lives of most Englishmen. In the past, it was a very different matter and, for instance, in 1784 William Pitt 'calculated that thirteen million pounds of tea were consumed in the Kingdom, of which only five and a half millions had paid duty'.[2] Tobacco, chinaware, lace, silks and plate-glass were brought in in a similar fashion, and the furnishing of the ducal mansion, Northumberland House, is only one of several known to have been accomplished by these means. At the time this was not looked upon as extraordinary, for the seizure of the goods on Cobb's premises apparently did not affect the success of his future trading. Confirmation of the general attitude is to be found in an entry in the diary of Lady Mary Coke, who congratulated herself on being unconventional in buying what she required and importing it openly. She noted in 1769:

> I've got my chairs from Paris, without being beholden to anybody; they have paid the duty, but I don't intend to have them covered with damask, or have the frames gilt, till after I return from abroad.

Lady Mary's mention of having her purchases gilded at a future date confirms a suspicion that chairs came across the Channel in an unfinished state. It is known that they arrived in pieces, for among the goods reported as seized from Walle and Reilly and James Cullen were:

76 Chair Fronts complete.
74 Single Back Feet, one of which is broke.

10 Backs put together.
16 Stumps and Side Rails joined.
87 Chairs unput together.
6 Large Sophas unput together.

When 'unput together' they could not have been gilt, or the fragile gesso and gold leaf would certainly have been damaged during transit or when being assembled. They reached this country, therefore, in pieces and with untreated surfaces. In 1778 a visitor to Heythrop House, Oxfordshire, remarked on the drawing-room, which the owner's wife, the Countess of Shrewsbury, said cost £6,000 to furnish,

> . . . the two sofas ninety guineas each, each chair thirty. They are of tent stitch-work at Paris, the carved frames made there and gilt in England.[3]

Doubtless the custom of having such articles gilded on arrival at their destination was taken for granted, and thus there are very few references to its having taken place.

Another occupant of premises in St. Martin's Lane was, like Cobb, engaged in smuggling and shared the misfortune of being caught, although not in the same fashion. Thomas Chippendale, who had been in France in October of the preceding year (see page 14), was detected importing in 1769

> . . . one case containing, five Dozen of chairs, unfinished Value Eighteen pounds all (French) but that on Examination they [the Customs officers] have Reason to believe, the same is greatly under Valued, and have therefore stopped them for the Boards Directions. . . .

[1] See Geoffrey Wills, 'Furniture Smuggling in Eighteenth Century London', in *Apollo*, August 1965, and William Rieder, 'Furniture-Smuggling for a Duke', in *Apollo*, September 1970.

[2] G. M. Trevelyan, *English Social History*, 1944, page 387.

[3] *Passages from the Diaries of Mrs. Philip Lybbe Powys* (ed. Emily J. Climenson), 1899, page 200, quoted by F. J. B. Watson, *Wallace Collection Catalogues: Furniture*, 1956, page 106.

Left, *Fig. 48: Underside view of the table in Plate 8, showing the three-way metal plate found beneath the majority of old tripod bases.* **Right,** *Plate 8: Mahogany tea table with an octagonal top and tripod base. Circa 1765; height 72 cm. (Private collection.)*

The Commissioners of Customs did not hesitate to take advantage of the law, by paying Chippendale the value at which he had declared the goods, £18, plus ten per cent, and keeping the chairs. There can be no doubt that they disposed of them advantageously.[1]

Among other cabinet-makers of the time were the Bradshaws, Paul Saunders, and Samuel Norman and James Whittle. The names of William Bradshaw and George Smith Bradshaw are recorded as having supplied furniture, but their relationship to to one another remains undiscovered. Saunders is known to have been in partnership with George Smith Bradshaw in 1756, when the two men delivered a quantity of goods to the Earl of Leicester at Holkham Hall, Norfolk. Saunders alone apparently then took over the Soho tapestry manufactory, which had been established in that part of London in 1685. It was noted in the press in September 1757 that he had been appointed 'Tapestry Maker to his Majesty', and in 1769 he was 'Yeoman Arras-worker and Arras-taylor' to the Great Wardrobe.

---

[1] Edward T. Joy, 'Chippendale in Trouble at the Customs', in *Country Life*, 24 August 1951.

A suite of six armchairs and a settee with walnut cabriole legs and upholstered in tapestry signed 'Bradshaw', was once at Belton House, Lincolnshire. Dating from about 1725 the covering was woven by George Smith Bradshaw, who is recorded also as having made large wall-tapestries. He provided some furniture for the Admiralty in 1764–74 and had a total of three different addresses in the Soho area between 1737 and 1787. Saunders, however, did not stay in Soho for many years and in 1763 moved away from the district.

It was announced in 1758 that James Whittle and Samuel Norman had acquired premises in King Street, Covent Garden, where they would 'carry on the Upholstery and Cabinet as well as the Carving and and Gilding Businesses in all their branches . . .'. Some years earlier they had been employed by the Earl of Cardigan, to make some tables and pier-glasses, but by 1759 the partnership would seem to have terminated as Norman's name only is mentioned in a report in the *General Evening Post* of 25 December 1759 (No. 4087):

> Yesterday morning about four o'clock a terrible fire broke out at Mr. Norman's (late Mr. West's) an eminent Cabinet-maker, Carver and Gilder, in King-street, Covent-Garden, which entirely consumed that house, with the houses of Mr. Bellis, a Jeweller and Toyman on one side, and Mr. Fortescue, a linen draper on the other; and greatly damaged two others . . . it is computed that about thirty houses are consumed, and several more damaged.

The *Gentleman's Magazine* (Vol. XXIX,

page 605) stated that 50 houses had been destroyed and added that 'the loss is computed at more than £70,000'.

Accounts preserved at Woburn Abbey, Bedfordshire, show that Samuel Norman supplied goods and services in 1759 and 1760 to the fourth Duke of Bedford. The majority of the furniture remains in the house, but the curtains he made have had to be replaced. No doubt the same fate has befallen the bell wires which Norman's men repaired in October 1760. His bills at that date were addressed from 'The Royal Tapestry Manufactory, Soho Square', whence he had removed following the disaster in King Street.[1]

---

[1] For details of the furnishing of Woburn Abbey see Gladys Scott Thomson, *Family Background*, 1949.

Hundreds of other cabinet-makers lived and worked in the mid-18th Century, but their furniture remains unidentified and their existence is known only from brief entries in directories or from documents. A proportion of them employed printed trade-cards many of which were listed and illustrated by Sir Ambrose Heal. In spite of the use of the word 'Makes' on the example in Fig. 49, Daniel Wakelin was probably a retailer and orders he gained for new furniture were filled on his behalf by a working cabinet-maker. The distinction between 'dealer' and 'maker' was not always clearly observed in the past, and many of the tradesmen who stated they owned workshops did not in fact do so.

Fig. 49: Trade-card of Daniel Wakelin, dated 1763. (Photograph courtesy of The Connoisseur.)

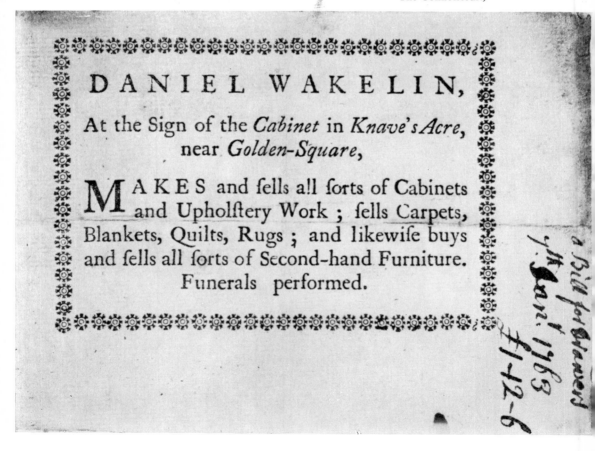

DANIEL WAKELIN,

At the Sign of the *Cabinet* in *Knave's Acre*, near *Golden-Square*,

MAKES and sells all sorts of Cabinets and Upholstery Work ; sells Carpets, Blankets, Quilts, Rugs ; and likewise buys and sells all sorts of Second-hand Furniture. Funerals performed.

a Bill for Glavers 7th Jan.t 1763 £1-42-6

5 : Ince, Mayhew, Manwaring & Johnson

THOMAS CHIPPENDALE's book was the first of its kind to be published, and it led the way for many others. Next in the field were William Ince and John Mayhew, who jointly set up in business in Broad Street, Soho, in January 1759. The two men had served their apprenticeships in London: Mayhew with George Smith Bradshaw, and Ince with John West. The latter had traded for many years in King Street, Covent Garden, and following his death in 1758 his premises were occupied by Samuel Norman (see page 62). Norman, together with James Whittle, had been partnered by John Mayhew when he bought the King Street lease, but Mayhew broke away very soon afterwards.

Only six months after Ince and Mayhew had established themselves in Soho, the *Gentleman's Magazine* (July 1759, vol. 29, page 338) listed under 'Books published':

A general system of useful and ornamental furniture. By Mess. Ince and Mayhew, publishing in numbers. 1s. each.

The parts were finally bound together and the whole issued in a single volume, undated but probably in 1762.

The Universal System of Household Furniture, as it is named, is a folio like the *Director*. Whereas that book has a plain type-set title-page, Ince and Mayhew gave theirs an elaborate engraved one of Rococo design signed 'W. Ince, inv^t. et delin.'. There follows a further essay in complex scroll-work, but this time the wording accompanying it is in French:

La Système Universel de Garniture de Maison.

Next is an engraved page headed by the coat of arms of George Spencer, fourth Duke of Marlborough, while beneath it is the dedication. Some of the copies have been amended and reveal the dates between which they were issued, for, following the Duke's titles are the words 'Lord Lieutenant & Custos Rotulorum of the County of Oxford'.[1] They are in script, but following them, crowded into a small vacant space

---

[1] The copy in the Victoria and Albert Museum Library bears the alteration to the dedication, and is the one used for the re-print published with a preface by Ralph Edwards, 1960.

Left, *Plate 9: Mahogany serpentine-fronted chest of drawers, the canted corners decorated with blind fret and the edge of the top, apron and feet carved with leaf and other ornament.* Circa 1770; width 110·5 cm. *(Private collection.)*

Above, *Fig. 50: 'Un Grand Sofa', designed by William Ince in a mixture of French, Chinese and Gothic styles. Engraving from* The Universal System. Circa 1760.

and in contrasting 'print' is '& Lord Chamberlain of his Majesties Houshold &c.'. The Duke, great-grandson of the famous General, was appointed Lord Chamberlain in November 1762, a few months later he became Lord Privy Seal, and had he held that appointment at the time it would certainly have appeared on the dedication page. Therefore Ince and Mayhew must have issued these copies of the bound version between November 1762 and April 1763, and the un-amended copies in the months prior to the first date.

The *Preface* to the book is followed by an *Explanation of the Plates*, the last being printed in two columns with English on the left and French on the right. The actual plates total 155, of which the first three are of Rococo foliage, two being signed by Ince

and engraved by Matthew Darly. The same engraver was responsible for the remaining plates, with the exception of a group of unsigned ones which are clearly by a less skilful hand. The designs themselves show variations of those made earlier by Chippendale, with the addition of tripod-based tea tables, entitled 'Claw Tables', which had appeared in the 1760 *Houshold Furniture* but not in any edition of the *Director*. Styles are the now-familiar mixture of French, Chinese and Gothic, with a considerable use of fret either 'blind' or pierced through.

Ince and Mayhew also contributed a score or so of unsigned designs to the various editions of *Houshold Furniture* (see page 32). They are recognisable from a close similarity to their counterparts in the

Universal System, but are unsigned and unremarkable.

In spite of the fact that the firm was in business in Broad Street for twenty years and then in Marshall Street, Westminster, for several more, very few of their productions have been positively identified. Both partners served for periods as directors of the Westminster Fire Office, to whom they supplied board-room chairs in 1793 and 1813 which remain today in the possession of the same insurance company. A mahogany boookcase in the Museum of Decorative Arts, Copenhagen, bears the printed label of Ince and Mayhew, probably affixed because the piece was made for export.[1] They also issued a printed invitation which stated:

> Mayhew & Ince respectfully announce that they have an Assortment of French Furniture, consign'd from Paris, for immediate Sale, very much under the original Cost, which may be seen at their Warehouse, Broad Street, Soho.

The above-mentioned pieces of furniture were certainly from the firm's workshops, but others which are less completely documented may have been made by other cabinet-makers following the designs in the book. A pair of large pier-glasses in the Metropolitan Museum of Art, New York, are in this category. They resemble closely one of the engravings bearing the legend 'W. Ince inv^t. et delin.' but their earlier provenance is obscure and no bills exist to authenticate them. In the same Museum is another large-sized glass originally in the Tapestry Room at Croome Court, Warwickshire, for which it was designed by Robert Adam. Ince and Mayhew supplied it to the Earl of Coventry in 1769, and their account described it as:

> A large Architect Pier Frame, fluted richly carv'd with shell on top, festoons and drops of double husks down the sides, goates heads at bottom gilt in the very best Double Burnish'd Gold . . . £35.[2]

It is uncertain whether the partners did their gilding on the premises or sub-contracted such work to a specialist. As regards the glass, a 1790 directory listed them as 'Upholders, Cabinet-Makers and Manufacturers of Plate Glass'. Here, again, doubts must be raised, for they may

---

[1] Illustrated in Ralph Edwards and Margaret Jourdain, *Georgian Cabinet-Makers*, third edition, 1955, pages 203–4.

[2] J. Parker, 'Croome Court, the Architecture and Furniture' in *Bulletin of the Metropolitan Museum of Art*, vol. XVIII (1959–60), pages 79–85. This glass and one of the pair previously mentioned illustrated in Geoffrey Wills, *English Looking-Glasses*, 1965, pages 104 and 123.

Left, *Fig. 51: Mahogany dressing-table, the frieze decorated with blind fret and the legs in the form of cluster columns. Circa 1760: width closed 58·4 cm.*

Below, *Fig. 52: The same table with the top open. (Colonial Williamsburg, Virginia: photograph John Keil, Ltd.)*

have been merely shareholders in a firm of glass-makers elsewhere, and implied otherwise for prestige. In any case, it is unlikely that they would have had furnaces in the middle of London, notwithstanding they were directors of a fire insurance company. That it would seem they had some connection with glass-making or finishing is clear from evidence given to a Parliamentary committee in 1773 by a Mr. 'John Mayo'; the latter without doubt a phonetic rendering of Mayhew. 'Mayo' then described himself as a cabinet-maker and 'Worker of Plate', which is a vague term. He did not mention making glass on his own account but said he had imported some from France.

It has been suggested from time to time that chairs bearing beneath their frames the branded initials I.M. were made by Ince and Mayhew. There is no positive proof either way, but the proposal would be more ac-ceptable if the mark was 'I. & M.'. Branding of this type is found from the late 17th Century onwards, but present evidence suggests it was employed by makers specialising in chairs and probably not by general cabinet-makers.

Whereas large businesses, like those of Chippendale and Ince and Mayhew would have made chairs on their own premises, there were a number of makers who did nothing other than chair-making. Among those who were active in this respect in the 1760's was Robert Manwaring, who followed the current trend by publishing a book of designs. It was given the descriptive title:

The Cabinet and Chair-Maker's Real Friend and Companion, or, The Whole System of Chair-Making made plain and easy.

It was published in 1765, and contained 40 plates engraved by Robert Pranker, a little-

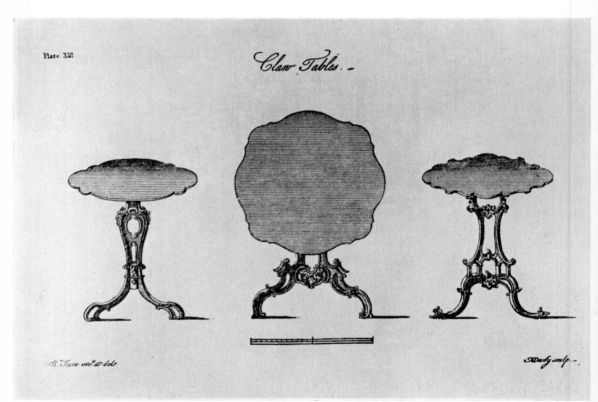

Plate XII   Claw Tables. -

known artist of what Redgrave termed 'mediocre class'. In his Preface Manwaring stated 'there are very few Designs advanced, but what he has either executed himself, or seen completely finished by others'. The five Orders of Architecture were illustrated, and there was also a plate showing 'the true Manner and Method of striking out all kind of Bevel Work relative to Chairs, by which the practical Workman will see at one View the Foundation Rules for obtaining his Art . . . by which the most ignorant Person will be acquainted at one View, with what many Artists have served Seven Years to know . . .'.[1]

The hundred designs for chairs include types for use on all occasions, and yet again make use of French, Chinese and Gothic motifs. The draughtsmanship is stiff and to the average eye has a complete lack of realism, but the author assures his readers that 'they will give general Satisfaction with respect to their Grandeur, Variety, Novelty and Usefulness'. A few chairs closely following Manwaring's designs have been recorded, but whether they came from his workshops is unknown. As was the case with Ince and Mayhew and some others, a few of Manwaring's designs were included in the 1760 and later editions of *Houshold Furniture*.

THE Rococo style, initiated in England as regards furniture by Matthias Lock and Henry Copland, reached its climax of expression in the work of Thomas Johnson. Whereas Chippendale and others usually displayed the style with a certain restraint, Johnson in most instances outdid the

---

[1] Manwaring's book was reprinted 1937.

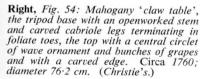

Left, *Fig. 53: 'Claw Tables' from Ince and Mayhew's* Universal System of Household Furniture. *Circa 1760.*

Right, *Fig. 54: Mahogany 'claw table', the tripod base with an openworked stem and carved cabriole legs terminating in foliate toes, the top with a central circlet of wave ornament and bunches of grapes and with a carved edge. Circa 1760; diameter 76·2 cm. (Christie's.)*

Left, *Fig. 55: Mahogany armchair with carved and pierced back and curved seat, related to one of Robert Manwaring's designs; in the present instance the top rail centres on the crest of the Connock family of Treworgey Manor, Cornwall. Circa 1760; height 94 cm. (Temple Newsam House, Yorkshire: Leeds City Art Gallery.)*

Above, *Fig. 56: 'Rural Chairs for Summer Houses', from* The Cabinet and Chair-Maker's Real Friend and Companion, *by Robert Manwaring, 1765.*

French in the audacity of his assymmetrical patterns. Curve linked with curve, foliage sprouted from crevices and corners, icicles and pinnacles were everywhere and, noticeably, there was an employment of human figures, animals and fishes.

To a late 19th-Century writer Johnson's designs appeared to be 'largely impracticable', but the shaft was mis-directed. Aldam Heaton, who also found Johnson's work commonplace and vulgar, used the words to describe what he thought was Chippendale's. In fact, an enterprising early 19th-Century publisher had possession of many of Johnson's original copper-plates, but he did not re-issue them as they were. He realised that Johnson's name was

then unknown but Chippendale's was remembered, so the name of Johnson was carefully removed from every single plate and that of Thomas Chippendale substituted. The fraud remained undetected until 1903, when the facts were published in order to restore the good name of Chippendale.[1] Thomas Johnson fared badly, and lapsed again into comparative obscurity for another forty years, when his designs were reprinted and his work subjected to a serious re-appraisal.[2]

[1] R. S. Clouston, 'Thomas Chippendale—Part III', in *The Connoisseur,* September 1903.

[2] Helena Hayward, *Thomas Johnson and English Rococo,* 1964.

Johnson was born in London in 1714, but there is no knowledge of how he learned his craft. By 1752 he was recorded as paying rates for premises off St. Giles's High Street, near the present-day junction of Tottenham Court Road and Charing Cross Road. Three years later, 'Thomas Johnson, Carver, in Queen Street near 7 Dials, London' published a four-sheet set of designs entitled *Twelve Gerandoles*. Each of them was engraved by William Austin, an artist who achieved only a moderate fame in his day and is probably most memorable for having died at the great age of 99 in 1820.

The girandoles, or wall-lights, are somewhat similar to those of Thomas Chippen-dale, but several of them incorporate in their design features taken from the illustrations to Aesop's *Fables* which had been executed by Francis Barlow in 1666. Thus, in the example in Fig. 60 the snarling boar is from Fable CII, 'The Boar and the Ass', although the ass is missing and the owl perched to one side and the Chinaman at the top are unconnected with the story.

Next, in the years 1756–7 Johnson brought out a series of plates in monthly parts, each of which comprised four engravings. They finally totalled 53, and were published in bound form in 1758 with the addition of a dedication plate to take the place of a title-page. The dedication was to

Below, *Fig. 57: Designs for candle-stands by Thomas Johnson, published in 150 New Designs, 1761. The right-hand one was used for the stand in Fig. 58.*

Right, *Fig. 58: Candle-stand of partly stained pinewood with metal arms, from a design by Thomas Johnson dated 1756. Circa 1760; height 157·5 cm. (Temple Newsam House, Yorkshire: Leeds City Art Gallery.)*

Lord Blakeney, defender of the island of Minorca against a French seige in 1756, who duly became Grand-President of the Anti-Gallican Society and was addressed as such by the author. Subtly emphasising the strongly patriotic nature of the work is the fact that it was issued on St. George's Day, April 23rd.

The fact that most of the designs lean heavily on French sources for their inspiration did not deter Johnson from adopting this attitude. Additionally, at the head of the plate is a small airborne angel holding in his hand a torch with which he is setting alight a paper scroll bearing the words 'French Paper Machee': a substance which was undoubtedly a threat to the livelihood of a wood-carver, and was a more tangible one than the popular liking for French-inspired designs.

The plates were engraved by three artists, of whom Butler Clowes was responsible for 41, James Kirk for five and William Austin for only one. Clowes has been noticed earlier as having executed some of the *Director* illustrations, James Kirk made a set of 32 copies of Barlow's Aesop plates, and Austin had earlier engraved the *Twelve Gerandoles*.

The book, which appeared minus a title-page and is usually referred to as 'Johnson's Collections of Designs, 1758', was published by the carver from a fresh address. This was

'At the Golden Boy, in Grafton Street, St. Ann's, Westminster'; a street which no longer exists but was situated in Soho to the west of the top of St. Martin's Lane. The volume was re-issued in 1761 by Robert Sayer, an extra plate was included and the whole entitled *One Hundred and Fifty New Designs*.

Two further publications are linked with

Johnson's name. Seven plates in *Houshold Furniture*, 1760, have been attributed to him, and there is a record of a volume entitled *A New Book of Ornaments by Thos. Johnson*, which was issued in 1760. Of this, only the title-page seems to have survived, but some of the plates themselves were more durable and were printed from in the 19th Century. As with others by Johnson they appeared with his name erased and that of Chippendale in its place.

There is little information about Thomas Johnson's carving. It seems that in addition to issuing his designs he was in business as a carver supplying others who dealt direct with private purchasers. In this way, it is thought he was responsible for looking-glass frames and console tables bought in 1761 and 1763 by the Duke of Atholl. They were for Dunkeld House and Blair Castle in Scotland, and the invoices which survive show that their supplier was a Londoner, George Cole, of Golden Square, who described himself as an 'Upholsterer'.

Cole also supplied furniture to Corsham Court, Wiltshire, between 1761 and 1763 and it is likely that Thomas Johnson was similarly concerned behind the scenes. Surviving furniture in the mansion includes a number of pieces which, like the purchases made by the Duke of Atholl, show features favoured by Johnson and seen in his printed designs.[1]

Directly following the design on a plate dated 1756 in Johnson's publication of 1758 is a well-known set of four candle-stands which were once at Hagley Hall, Worcestershire. They have since been divided and a pair is in the Philadelphia Museum of Art, one is in the Victoria and Albert Museum and the fourth is at Temple Newsam (Fig. 58). Each is carved in pine-wood partly

---

[1] See Anthony Coleridge, op. cit., pages 60 and 61, plates 99–113.

stained to simulate mahogany, and a comparable use of entwined dolphins was included by Chippendale in the third (1762) edition of the *Director*.

If, as is probable, Johnson was responsible for some of the furniture at Blair Castle and Corsham Court in 1763 the work would appear to have proved unprofitable to him. On 15th September 1764 the *London Gazette* printed an announcement that 'Thomas Johnson, of Store-street in the Parish of Saint Giles in the Fields in the County of Middlesex, Carver and Painter' was declared bankrupt. In the *Gentleman's Magazine* there was brief notice to the same effect but giving his trade as 'Painter', and to make honours even the *London Magazine* listed him as 'Carver'.[1] The cause and effects of this event are not known, but no further mentions of it appear to have been printed at the time.

Whether it was on account of his bankruptcy or for some other reason, Johnson has so far not been found to have made any further appearances of significance in the records of the time. It is known that in 1767 he relinquished one of two premises he leased in Tottenham Court Road, and that he continued in possession of the other until 1778. No later mention of him has yet come to light, and the date of his death remains to be discovered.

The stern opinions of Thomas Johnson's variety of Rococo voiced by the Victorian and later critics are less often heard today, and he occupies the position of a man who brought the style to full manifestation. Within a decade of his *Twelve Gerandoles* in 1755 the neo-classical was fast being supplanted in public favour by the Rococo,

Above, *Fig. 62: Armchair of the same design as the side chair in Fig. 61.* Circa *1760. (Phillips, Son & Neale.)*

which perhaps explains why the man who was so fully committed to the old succumbed to utter obscurity in the face of the new.

[1] *Gentleman's Magazine*, September 1764 (vol. 34, page 451); *London Magazine*, do. (vol. 33, page 487).

6 : *Adam, Langlois, & the Linnells*

A REVIVAL of interest in the styles of ancient Greece and Rome led to the emergence of a complete antithesis to the Rococo. The voluptuous curves, asymmetry and random ornament of the latter were supplanted by a comparatively austere and precise placing of carefully drawn elements duly known as the neo-classical style. Its adoption in England was due to the Scottish architect, Robert Adam, who returned from his foreign travels in 1758.

Classical ornament had held an appeal for a minority from quite early in the 18th Century. The ceilings of the Presence Chamber at Kensington Palace, London, and of the Smoking Room at Rousham, Oxford, designed by William Kent in about 1725 and 1735, respectively, show an orderly employment of winged griffins, terms and vases linked by festoons of husks, leaves and ribbons.[1] They pre-dated the event which aroused the whole of Europe to remembering and studying the near-forgotten past: the discovery and excavation of the buried remains of Herculaneum and Pompeii.

The two cities, situated close to Naples in the south of Italy, were tragically overwhelmed by an eruption of Vesuvius in A.D. 79. The disaster killed the majority of their inhabitants, but preserved the buildings and their contents beneath a layer of volcanic ash and stones of varying depth. All lay undisturbed until early in the 18th Century, when a search for stone to make plaster for building a mansion in the vicinity of Herculaneum revealed that the peasants had been digging up marble blocks and statues for some years past. Serious excavations began in about 1738, but it was a further period of years before the results were published in any detail. Pompeii was located in 1748, but again there was considerable delay and it was 1763 before systematic exploration commenced.

---

[1] Illustrated in Francis Lenygon (Margaret Jourdain), *Decoration in England from 1660–1770*, (1914), figs. 177–8.

In London, members of the Royal Society heard a little about some of the early discoveries in 1743, which reached a wider public through the *Gentleman's Magazine* (Vol. 13, pages 472 and 586). Finds of gold, bronze and brass objects were reported, as well as thirty paintings which were, readers were told:

> Such Pictures as were never seen in our Days; quite surprizing—Painting finish'd to the highest Pitch, colour'd to Perfection, and as fresh as if they had been done a Month ago.

The events were eagerly followed in every country, and a debate duly ensued as to the relative superiority of Roman or Greek art. In this, the chief protagonist in favour of the Greeks was Johann Joachim Winckelmann, a German shoemaker's son who made an intensive study of classical art and literature. In 1762 he went to Rome where he was appointed librarian to a Cardinal, embraced the Roman Catholic faith and was known thenceforward as the Abbé Winckelmann. Two years later he published the first reliable account of the finds made at Herculaneum and Pompeii.

One of the Abbé's books on Grecian painting and sculpture was translated into English by the Swiss, Johann Heinrich Fussli, newly arrived in London, who later anglicised his name to Henry Fuseli and in time became professor of painting at the Royal Academy. The opening words of the

Left, *Plate 11: Pier table and glass: the frame of the latter closely following a design by Robert Adam dated 1769; the table of which no design survives, made by Joseph Parfetti. Circa 1770; width 172·7 cm. (Saltram, Devon: The National Trust.)*

Below, *Fig. 63: Designs for a side table, urns and pedestals, two ewers and a wine cooler, by Robert Adam. Circa 1780.*

essay pronounce the doom of all that was not of Hellenic origin:

> To the Greek climate we owe the production of TASTE, and from thence it spread at length over all the politer world.[1]

ROBERT ADAM was the second of the four sons of a Scottish architect, William Adam, and after some years of schooling studied at Edinburgh University where he matriculated in 1743. At first he worked in his father's office as an assistant and in due course tackled projects of his own inspiration. When William Adam died in 1748, Robert joined with his elder brother, John, in managing the practice.

In 1754, at the age of 26, Robert Adam set forth on his travels, his Grand Tour commencing with a short stay in France. A year later he was in Florence and in 1765 went on to Rome. He was not there for very long, for on 11th July 1757 he set sail from

Venice in company with some friends on an expedition to Split, on the coast of Dalmatia. The purpose of the journey was to measure and draw the ruins of the ancient palace of Diocletian, the Roman Emperor who died in the 4th Century A.D. The task was accomplished with difficulty, because the local authorities viewed the enterprise with the suspicion invariably reserved everywhere for foreigners who could as easily be spies as archaeologists.

A brief stay in Italy was followed by a return through the Rhineland to England,

---

[1] *Reflection on the Painting and Sculpture of the Greeks: with Instructions for the Connoisseur, and an Essay on Grace in Works of Art*, 1765.

Above, *Fig. 65: Pair of armchairs, belonging to the same suite as the settee in Fig. 64 and the firescreen in Fig. 67. Circa 1770. (All in the Philadelphia Museum of Art: photographs Christie's.)*

and early in 1758 Robert Adam was settled in London. Together with his two sisters, joined later by his brother James when the latter returned from his Grand Tour, he established himself in Lower Grosvenor Street in a most fashionable area of the city.

Alongside Adam in introducing the neo-classic style, but lacking the essential drive to make the most of his talents and opportunities, was a fellow-Scot, James Stuart. In 1751, in company with a friend, he visited Greece, and eleven years later they produced jointly a volume of engravings en-titled *The Antiquities of Athens*. As a result, Stuart achieved not only fame as an authority on classical forms but was known ever afterwards by the nick-name 'Athenian'. While he did not lack commissions for both buildings and their interior decoration, he was a contrast to Adam in temperament being indolent as regards work and careless over money.[1]

Stuart began working on the decoration of Spencer House, St. James's, soon after Adam arrived in London, but the latter did not have to wait long for his first important commission. Sir Nathaniel Curzon, later Lord Scarsdale, chose Robert Adam to modify and complete his mansion, Kedle-ston, Derbyshire, which had been begun by James Paine. For the interior Adam provided not only the still-existing decoration, but he designed a number of pieces of furniture for the principal rooms. From then onwards he provided a steady flow of drawings for whatever was required by his clients.

[1] H. M. Colvin, *Biographical Dictionary of British Architects*, 1954.

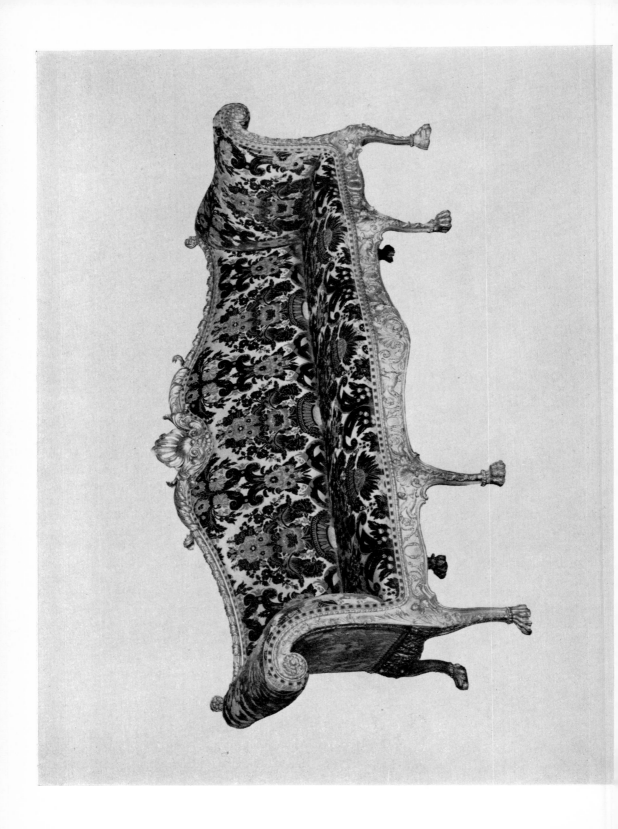

Robert Adam died in 1792 followed two years later by his brother James, and in 1822 by the youngest, William. Prior to this last date there had been auction-sales of the possessions of both Robert and James, but these included only a proportion of their drawings. The majority of them, numbering nearly nine thousand, were purchased in 1833 by Sir John Soane, the architect, and remain in his Museum in Lincoln's Inn Fields, London.[1]

Modern research has demonstrated that Robert Adam's reputation as a designer of furniture had grown inflated with time, and the assumed quantity could not be substantiated. Only in a very few instances did he undertake the furnishing of other than the principal rooms of mansions, and in the main his share was limited to such objects as looking-glass frames which might be considered more as fixtures and therefore part of the fabric.[2]

One of Adam's most important and best documented commissions was for the decoration and furnishing of the houses in Arlington Street, London, and Moor Park, Hertfordshire, belonging to Sir Lawrence Dundas. One of the features at Moor Park was a room hung with specially-commissioned Gobelins tapestry, and furnished with a giltwood suite of chairs and settees upholstered to match the hangings. When the house was demolished in 1785 the room was dismantled and installed at Arlington Street, and in 1934 the latter, in turn, succumbed to progress. On that occasion the tapestries were retained by the descendants of Sir Lawrence, but the movables were sold.

The tapestry-covered suite comprised three settees, ten armchairs, a pair of window seats and four firescreens, and most of the pieces are now in the Philadelphia Museum of Art (Fig. 64). The drawings for them have not survived, and although Robert Adam's name has been quoted in this connection it is now thought unlikely that he was concerned with their design. A recent discovery has brought to light the information that the makers of the suite were some hitherto unrecorded cabinet-makers: Samuel Fell and William Turton.[3]

---

[1] The drawings are indexed in Arthur T. Bolton, *The Architecture of Robert and James Adam*, 2 vols., 1922, vol. II. The furniture designs are also listed in Eileen Harris, *The Furniture of Robert Adam*, 1963, page 47.

[2] Eileen Harris, op. cit., page 25.

[3] Eileen Harris, 'The Moor Park Tapestries', in *Apollo*, September 1967, page 180.

Left, *Fig. 66: Carved giltwood settee, from a suite of eight armchairs and four settees, designed by Robert Adam in 1764 and made by Thomas Chippendale.* (*Sotheby's.*) **Below**, *Fig. 67: Firescreen belonging to the suite illustrated in Figs. 64 and 65.*

One of their accounts, dated 1771, included the following:

> To 2 sophas carved and gilt in Burnished gold. Stuff'd with Best curl'd hair and fine linnen ... £25 each   50. –. –.
>
> To covering d° with your Tapistrey, used Brass naills, sewing silk fine Durrant for the Backs tax etc.[1]   1. 10. –.

Sir Lawrence Dundas also purchased another giltwood suite, this one comprising eight armchairs and four settees. Adam's original design for them is in Sir John Soane's Museum, while his charge for the work reads:

> To Design of sopha [and] Chairs for the Salon   5. –. –.

The same recent research that revealed the existence of Fell and Turton also found the completely unsuspected maker of this second suite: Thomas Chippendale. Sir Lawrence expended with him the sum of £1,123. 1s. 6d. between July 1763 and

---

[1] Durant or Durrant: a worsted cloth usually with a glazed finish. Tax: tacks.

Below, Fig. 68: One of a pair of commodes in the French taste as regards shape but inlaid with neo-classical ornament in various woods on a tulip-wood ground. Circa 1775; width 94 cm. (Sotheby's.)

January 1766. The account for the suite (Fig. 66), which was submitted by 'Thomas Chippendale and the Executor of James Rannie', reads:

8 large Arm Chairs exceeding Richly Carv'd in the Antick manner and Gilt in oil Gold Stuff'd and cover'd with your own Damask—and strong castors on the feet	160. 0. 0.
8 leather cases to ditto lin'd with flannel	8. 8. 0.
8 Crimson Check cases to Ditto	6. 0. 0.
4 large Sofas exceeding Rich to match the chairs	216. 0. 0.
4 leather covers to Ditto lin'd with flannel	12.12. 0.
4 cheque cases to Ditto	7. 4. 0.[1]

Sir Lawrence Dundas also employed other cabinet-makers, which suggests strongly that he was free to please himself as to who carried out Adam's designs. The latter would seem to have submitted his share of the work to his various clients, who then commissioned the execution as they wished.

---

[1] Anthony Coleridge, op. cit., page 122.

Below, Fig. 69: One of a pair of marquetry commodes in the style of Peter Langlois. Circa 1765; width 108 cm. (Sotheby's.)

Peter (Pierre) LANGLOIS was a link between the Rococo and the neo-classic. While the outlines of his furniture frequently conform to the earlier style, his proficiency at inlaying was a portent. During the 1760's inlay completely replaced carving for the ornamentation of most types of furniture. At first the designs employed were principally arrangements of floral sprays in the earlier French manner, but they were duly replaced by inspiration from the neo-classic repertoire.

Below, *Fig. 70: Design for a cabinet, by John Linnell. Drawing in pen and ink and watercolour. (Victoria and Albert Museum.)*

Right, *Fig. 71: Parcel-gilt mahogany cabinet resembling the design by John Linnell in Fig. 70. Circa 1775; width about 112 cm. (Mallett & Son Ltd.)*

An immigrant to London from Paris, Langlois arrived by 1759 and established himself in premises in Tottenham Court Road, near Windmill Street. His bi-lingual engraved trade-card shows a Rococo frame with Cupids and Fame disporting themselves amidst a clock, a table and a three-drawer commode. The latter is of curved outline, inlaid and with metal mounts, which accords with an entry in a directory published in 1763. It says of him.

> This artist performs all sorts of curious Inlaid Work, particularly Commodes in the foreign taste inlaid with Tortoise-shell, Brass, etc.

Some of the pieces made by Langlois have been identified within the past decade, and quite a number of them bear a resemblance to the example illustrated in Fig. 73. It is one of a pair sold at Christie's in 1966, and they are authenticated by a letter written two centuries earlier, in March 1763. The writer was Caroline, Lady Holland, who was discussing with her sister the making of a gift to the third member of the family:

> I hear she [the third of the sisters] likes L'Anglay's inlaid things very much, and I should wish to send her something that might suit one of her rooms, whether the commode table, bureau or *coins*, which to be sure one might vulgarly call corner cupboards, but really they are lovely and finish a room so well.

Predictably, some of Langlois's pieces are easily mistaken for French, especially those with elaborately patterned gilt metal mounts in the Louis XV style. A distinguishing feature often takes the form of a wood top, veneered and inlaid to match the body of the article, in place of the marble slab which is ever-present on true French pieces. In contradiction to this, a pair of commodes at Woburn Abbey, attributed to Langlois and of severe neo-classical form, have tops of *pietre dure*.

Published references to the activities of Pierre Langlois are confined to the years

1759–66, and so far nothing is known for certain of his later activities. It has been suggested that he may have been the Pierre-Eloi Langlois who is recorded as having become *maître-menuisier* in 1774 in Paris, and who died there in November 1805. As the London Langlois was a maker of veneered pieces and therefore an *ébéniste* it may be questioned whether he would have possessed the different skills by which to qualify as a *menuisier*. In the latter capacity he would have confined his attention to carved work, principally chairs and settees, and, in fact the stamp of P-E. Langlois is noted as having been found on such pieces.[1]

---

[1] François de Salverte, *Les Ebénistes du XVIII Siècle*, Paris, 4th edition, 1953.

Below, *Fig. 72: Japanned commode designed and made by John Linnell for the Chinese Bedroom at Badminton, Gloucestershire. Circa 1755; width 142·2 cm. (Victoria and Albert Museum: photograph Christie's.)*

Right, *Fig. 73: One of a pair of marquetry commodes made by Peter Langlois. Circa 1763; width 99·7 cm. (Christie's.)*

Recent years have seen the veil lifted a little from some portion of Langlois's life, but rather more has been revealed about a firm that was active for far longer than he was; that of William and John Linnell. The investigation of legal documents bearing on the will of John Linnell has been followed by the publication of the important collection of his original designs which are in the Victoria and Albert Museum.[1]

From these sources the business of the two men, who had premises in Berkeley Square, has been shown to have ranked with the foremost of their time in London.

William Linnell was born in the first years of the 18th Century and in 1717 began serving his apprenticeship with a joiner. Twelve years later he became a freeman of the Joiners' Company, and it is known that between 1739 and 1752 he was supplying furniture to Sir Richard Hoare, of Barn Elms, Surrey. Likewise, from 1749 onwards he numbered among his clients William Drake, of Grosvenor Square, London, and Shardeloes, Buckinghamshire. William Linnell died in 1763 and his stock-in-trade was sold by auction but his son, John, took over the business and continued to run it from the same premises as before. From details given in court at the time it would appear that the Linnells' employees numbered about the same as those of Chippendale, and there was a comparable variety of specialist departments.

Both the Linnells were accomplished carvers, so it is not surprising to find that they had workshops for carving and for gilding. There was also a glass store, but this would probably have been no more than a stock-room. Among a list of debts are three to glass-grinders which total just over £240, but while bevelling and polishing were sub-contracted it is not unlikely that silvering was done on the premises.

The drawings in the Victoria and Albert Museum range from chairs and tables to complete sides of rooms, and many of them bear the names of clients for whom it may

[1] Patricia Anne Kirkham, 'The Careers of William and John Linnell', in *Furniture History* III (1967), page 29. *Funiture History* V (1969), is devoted almost entirely to 'The Drawings of John Linnell', edited by Helena Hayward.

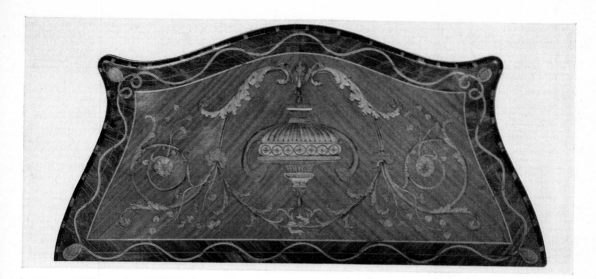

be assumed they were prepared and possibly executed. With their assistance it has been possible to name the Linnells as the designers and makers of the suite of japanned Chinese-style furniture once in the Chinese Bedroom at Badminton, Gloucestershire.[1] The most important of the pieces is the bed which, with the remainder, has always in the past been allocated to Thomas Chippendale as typical of his imaginative designs and best workmanship.

John Linnell's drawings show pieces in the styles which were current when they were executed, and include not only some with an Oriental appearance, but others with Rococo and many with neo-classic features. He is assumed to have been born in about 1737 and his surviving designs date from about 1755, when he was perhaps 18 years old, to about the year of his death, 1796. His passing was recorded briefly in the pages of the *Gentleman's Magazine* for April of that year (Vol. 66, part i, page 354).

March 27 At his house in Berkeley-square, Mr. John Linnell, upholder.

---

[1] Helena Hayward, 'Chinoiserie at Badminton', in *Apollo*, August 1969, page 134.

7 : Hepplewhite, Gillow & Others

WHILE a number of outstanding mansions were built, re-constructed or re-decorated in the neo-classical style, either by Robert Adam or one of his several followers, many people took a middle course in furnishing their more modest homes.

Below, Fig. 75: *Mahogany armchair, the shield-shaped back carved with the Prince of Wales' feathers.* Circa 1785. (*John Keil, Ltd.*)

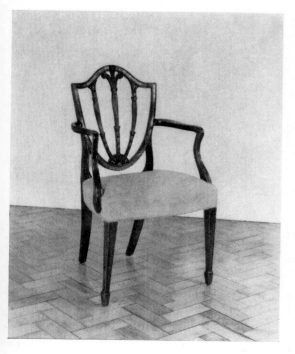

They did not go so far as Horace Walpole in condemning 'Mr. Adam's gingerbread and sippets of embroidery', but they wanted articles that were functional and unostentatious. A general idea of what was available can be gained from a study of the books of engravings published from the late 1780's onwards.

George Hepplewhite was a cabinet-maker with premises in Redcross Street, Cripplegate, in the City of London, but little further information about him or his activities has been recorded. Following his death in 1786 his widow, Alice, continued the business under the style of A. Hepplewhite and Co., although the names of her partners are unknown. She was responsible for issuing in 1788 a book of designs. *The Cabinet-Maker and Upholsterer's Guide.*[1]

The Preface to the book opens with a statement of the modest and laudable

---

[1] The third edition of 1794 is reprinted, with an Introduction by Joseph Aronson, published in New York by Dover Publications, Inc., and in London by Constable, 1969.

intentions of the writer, whoever he or she may have been.

To unite elegance and utility, and blend the useful with the agreeable, has ever been considered a difficult, but an honourable task. How far we have succeeded in the following work it becomes us not to say, but rather to leave it, with all due deference, to the determination of the public at large.

The designs include all kinds of articles, and while many of the pieces clearly incorporate neo-classical motifs, either carved, inlaid or painted, others are purely functional and almost devoid of any ornament whatsoever. Closely linked with Hepplewhite's name are chairs with shield-shaped backs, for which quite a number of designs are given.

The Prince of Wales, future King George IV, had attained his majority in 1783, and was then assigned Carlton House, Pall Mall, as a residence. It had been without a tenant since 1772, when it became empty following the death of the widow of Frederick Louis, the Prince of Wales who had himself died in 1751.

Prince George immediately set about altering the exterior and the interior of the mansion to suit his taste. Work was prosecuted with all haste and early in 1784, only a matter of six months after his twenty-

Left, *Plate 13: Painted satinwood cabinet with a central paned door flanked by mirror-fronted cupboards. Circa 1780; width about 140 cm. (H. Blairman & Sons.)*

Below, *Fig. 76: Carved mahogany side table based on a design in Hepplewhite's* Guide. *Circa 1790; width 164·5 cm. (Private collection.)*

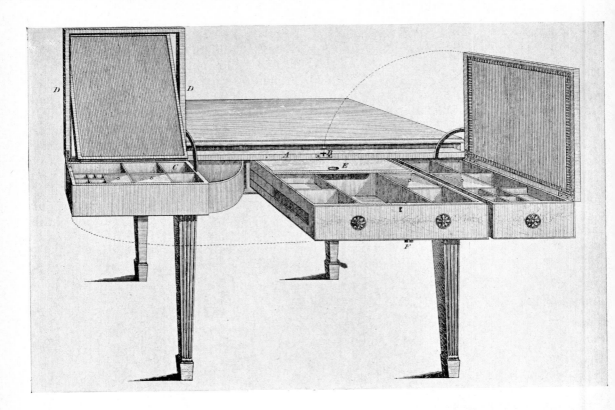

Above, *Fig. 77: Hepplewhite's design for Rudd's Table, dated 1787.*

first birthday, the Prince gave his first ball at Carlton House. The event was reported with polite enthusiasm in the *Gentleman's Magazine* (Vol. 54, part i, page 227):

> Wednesday 10 [March]. The elegant suite of apartments, lately fitted up at Carlton-house, were opened for the reception of a select party of the friends of the Prince of Wales. The visitants were of the first rank and distinction. The suite of rooms from the saloon to the ball-room, when the doors were opened, formed one of the grandest spectacles of the kind that was ever seen in this country.

Other periodicals noticed the event in similar terms.

The decoration and furnishing of the house was by no means completed by that date, and in 1786 a sum of £38,000 had been spent. Three years later, Robert Campbell, cabinet-maker, of Little Marylebone Street, Golden Square, was estimated to be owed no less than £10,500.[1] Understandably, Camp-

bell's colleagues, many of them possibly working for him on a contract basis, as well as his rivals, were eager to catch the Royal eye and attract money from the Royal purse —even if the latter was frequently empty and the payment of accounts long delayed.

With this in mind it is not unpredictable to find Hepplewhite casting a sidelong glance towards Pall Mall, and printing a few designs incorporating the Prince of Wales's feathers. One of them is a domed four-post bedstead, with the back surmounted by the Royal coat of arms and the three plumes. In other instances the backs of chairs centre on bold representations of the same badge. Of an armchair with

---

[1] H. Clifford Smith, *Buckingham Palace*, 1931, page 98.

Above, *Fig. 78: Rudd's Table, made by Thomas Scott, 29, Ludgate Hill.* Circa *1790; width closed 108·6 cm.* (*Christie's.*)

curved arms springing from almost the very top of the back, the printed comment reads: '... the arms ... though much higher than usual, have been executed with good effect for his Royal Highness the Prince of Wales'. Nevertheless, there is no mention in the Carlton House accounts of Hepplewhite's name, and if he made the chairs himself they must have been delivered and invoiced by someone else.

The side table illustrated in Fig. 76 shows many of the features of one in the *Guide*, and was probably inspired by the engraving. Its maker is unknown, whereas the dressing table in Figs. 79 and 80 bears the printed label of Thomas Scott, 29 Ludgate Hill, London, who was at that address from about 1783 to 1796. The design for it (Fig. 77) is given by Hepplewhite, where it is named and described as follows:

Rudd's Table, or Reflecting Dressing Table. This is the most complete dressing table made, possessing every convenience which can be wanted or mechanism and ingenuity supply. It derives its name from a once popular character, for whom it is reported it was first invented. The middle drawer of this table slides by itself—the two end drawers are framed to the slide A, and fasten at the catch B; and when disengaged, each drawer swings horizontally on a centre pin at C, and may be placed in any station as shewn in the drawing. The glasses turn upward, and are supported by a spring at the bottom of the quadrant, which pushed in, they fall down and slide under with the two end drawers. They also swing on the pins DD. E is a slide covered with green cloth for writing on; F the bolt of the lock, which shoots into the lower rail.

The 'once popular character' who gave her name to this ingenious piece of furniture was presumably Margaret Caroline

Rudd, who was tried for forgery at the Old Bailey in 1775. Her companions, two brothers named Perreau, were convicted and hanged, but Mrs. Rudd gained an acquittal and according to the *Annual Register* 'There were the loudest applauses on this acquittal almost ever known in a court of justice'. Her subsequent gay but short career as a courtesan terminated with her death in poverty in 1779.

The Gillow family of cabinet-makers originated in Lancashire, where Robert Gillow was made a freeman of the borough of Lancaster in 1728. Daniel Defoe visited there just before that date and wrote a somewhat depressing description of the place.

[It is] situate near the Mouth of the River Lone or Lune. The Town is antient; it lies, as it were, in its own Ruins, and has little to recommend it but a decayed Castle, and a more decayed Port (for no Ships of any considerable Burthen); the Bridge is handsome and strong, but, as before, here is little or no Trade, and few People.

Below, *Fig. 79: Mahogany dressing table stamped GILLOWS LANCASTER. Circa 1790: width closed about 90 cm. (John Keil, Ltd.)*

Just half a century later a change had occurred and Thomas Pennant was able to note that Lancaster was 'famous in having some very ingenious cabinet-makers settled here, who fabricate most excellent and neat goods at remarkably cheap rates, which they export to London and the plantations'.[1]

It is known that Gillow sent furniture to places as far apart as Riga and the West Indies, and in 1757, Robert's son, Richard, became a partner in the firm. In 1760 an establishment was opened in London, and by 1783 a directory entry referred to 'Robert, Richard and James Gillow, upholstery warehouse, 176 Oxford Street'. James Gillow was a cousin, and it was to him in 1760 that a letter was sent from the manufactory in the north requesting the supply of some of Thomas Chippendale's designs.

Two factors give a special interest to the furniture made by the firm. From some time in the 1790's they followed the French custom of putting their name to their productions by stamping each with a lettered

[1] *Tour in Scotland*, 1776, quoted by Edwards and Jourdain, op. cit., page 84.

Below, *Fig. 80: Rudd's Table opened. It is veneered with mahogany and crossbanded with tulip-wood. (Christie's.)*

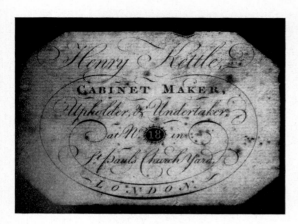

Above, *Fig. 81: Henry Kettle's printed label in the drawer of the table in Fig. 82. 6·4×15 cm.* **Right,** *Fig. 82: Inlaid Pembroke table by Henry Kettle, London. Circa 1780; width 75 cm. (Saltram, Devon: The National Trust.)*

steel punch. On the top edge of a drawer or elsewhere in an unobtrusive position is found either GILLOWS or GILLOWS LANCASTER. The firm continued to flourish into the 20th Century (the name is still to be seen in Oxford Street), and because of this fact dealers sometimes cut away the impressed name in case their clients thought the furniture was of recent manufacture.

Secondly, a very considerable quantity of the firm's records have been preserved, and are now in the City of Westminster Public Library, Buckingham Palace Road. The various documents run to nearly two hundred volumes, and include the private books in which are drawings and other details concerning each client's order. These, the Estimate Books, cover the years 1784 to 1905, and are 'a unique record of a large and successful firm of furniture-makers over two centuries'.[1]

A German visitor to England in the early 19th Century recorded a visit he made to Gillow's showrooms. He wrote of the firm as 'the first grade salesmen and manufacturers in London; they deal widely in

different parts of England; their work is good and solid, though not of the first class in inventiveness and style'.[2] It is the consistently good workmanship and well-selected timber rather than novelty of design that has ensured the survival of a fair quantity of their output. A detail favoured by the firm, although possibly not exclusive to him, is the use of a bail handle with angled ends and octagonal pins and plates. These are often found in conjunction with the stamped mark, as on the dressing table in Fig. 79.

A number of cabinet-makers of the time are known today because of the fortunate survival of some of their labelled pieces. In some instances the small printed papers have been overlooked and have come to light only recently. The table in Fig. 82 bears the label of Henry Kettle (Fig. 81) inside the drawer. It was found there completely by chance during repairs, after the drawer had remained unopened for uncounted years. At some date in the past one of the table's legs had been broken near the top, and a hasty repair was made by putting a long screw through the leg into the frame. It went un-noticed that the screw, while providing rigidity also went into the side of the drawer and made it immovable. The table remained in this condition until a more careful attempt at repairing it was made, and when this took place the maker's name was revealed. As the label had been so effectively shielded from daylight, dust and wear and tear for a long time, it is in remarkably good order.

Kettle's label has been discovered on a

---

[1] Nicholas Goodison and John Hardy, 'Gillows at Tatton Park', in *Furniture History* VI, 1970, page 1.

[2] P. A. Nemmich, *Neuste Reise durch England*, 1807, quoted by Edwards and Jourdain, op. cit., page 86.

Above, *Fig. 83: Printed label of Philip Bell of St. Paul's Church Yard, London, in a drawer of the chest shown in Plate 9. 14·6 × 9·5 cm.*

Right, *Fig. 84: Mahogany secretaire-bookcase made by Henry Kettle (see Fig. 81.) Circa 1780; width 106·7 cm. (Saltram, Devon: The National Trust.)*

number of other pieces of furniture including a table with an oval inlaid in the top, giving it a similar appearance to the Pembroke table just mentioned. A further example is the secretaire-cabinet in Fig. 84. It is of mahogany with the applied carving on the cornice executed in boxwood, the two upper drawers in the lower part being shams concealing a writing space.

Henry Kettle's premises were at 18 St. Paul's Churchyard between about 1774 and 1777, and he then removed to No. 23. The earlier address had previous to his tenure been occupied by another cabinet-making family named Bell. Known in pre-numbering days as *The White Swan*, it was in the possession of Henry Bell from about 1736

until 1750, after which Elizabeth Bell, presumably Henry's widow was there. A few years later her label bore an added '& Son', and from about 1786, the son, Philip Bell took over the business entirely. Prior to the coming of Henry Bell, another firm of cabinet-makers, Coxed and Wooster, had been at the *White Swan*, so that the premises were used by members of the same trade throughout the whole of the 18th Century.

A few pieces of furniture labelled by the various members of the Bell family have been recorded by Heal (op. cit., pages 6, 13–14, and 252–3), and the chest of drawers illustrated in Plate 9 can now be added to them. The label in the top drawer is shown in Fig. 83. In design and wording it is exactly the same as that of Henry Bell, except for the different forename. The wording at the foot, torn in the present example, should read:

N.B. Old Glasses new Worked & made up Fashionable.

It is an offer to alter the size and style of framing of old looking-glasses so as to bring them up to date, a useful service in view of the fact that the glass then cost considerably more than its surround.

Philip Bell's label had done service for a considerable time, but some while after he had acquired the business he put his name to a freshly designed one. It was engraved for him, and perhaps also designed, by Matthew Darly, and depicts the white swan seated on its nest above a Rococo frame flanked by an armchair and a Chinese cabinet. The offer to re-furbish glasses was omitted and in its place is the brief statement:

N.B. Funerals Perform'd.

There was nothing unusual in an 18th-Century cabinet-maker or upholder furnishing funerals. Heal illustrates the trade card of William Clarkson, of Moorfields, who describes himself as 'Upholder, Appraiser, Cabinet-Maker & Undertaker',

Above, *Fig. 85: Brass-bound mahogany wine cooler with a carved gadrooned rim and four-legged stand, made by a maker who specialised in such articles. Circa 1780; width 71 cm. (Stourhead, Wiltshire: The National Trust.)*

Above, *Fig. 86: Mahogany wing bookcase, the centre drawer fitted as a secretaire. Circa 1780; width about 240 cm. (Private collection: photograph* The Connoisseur.)

Right, *Fig. 87: Cabinet on stand decorated with marquetry on a satinwood ground. Circa 1780; width 62·9 cm. (Saltram, Devon: The National Trust.)*

adding 'Estates, Stocks in Trade, and Houshold Furniture, Bot & Sold'. Clarkson was not alone in providing such varied services, while at the same date, *circa* 1785, Thomas Silk, of St. Paul's Churchyard, illustrated on his card a funeral procession with black-gowned bearers and plumed, black-draped coffin approaching the steps of a church or chapel. Coffins, indeed, were supplied also by Gillows of Lancaster, and there are sketches and specifications of them in the firm's Estimates Books.

The use of the terms 'upholder' and 'cabinet-maker' would appear to have been indiscriminate in the past, and as has been mentioned in these pages a man sometimes styled himself 'cabinet-maker' when it is probable that he did not actually *make* goods but was only a retailer. Dr. Johnson gives upholder as synonymous with under-

taker, which further confuses the picture, and the precise status of most of the members of the furnishing trade at the time will possibly never be clarified.

Some years prior to the date of publication of Hepplewhite's *Guide* the appointment of cabinet-maker to the King was held by John Bradburn, who was succeeded in 1777 by William Gates. Bradburn had been in the employ of Vile and Cobb and some of his identified pieces resemble theirs in the use of carefully selected veneers and high quality carving. Some of his furniture is still at Buckingham Palace, supplied when it was known as the Queen's House, and in 1767 he was called on to provide his Royal clients with a 'Chamber Horse':

. . . to carry 4 children at once, with a mahogany frame and spring seats all round with morocco leather . . . with 4

handles . . . and made to turn on a swivel, and 4 footboards made to fall down occasionally for the Conveniency of carrying it through any doorway.[1] This attractive-sounding contrivance cost £10. 15s. and was delivered for the use of the occupants of the 'Nursery at the Queen's House'. No doubt it had plenty of usage, for it would seem to have been discarded long ago.

The furniture supplied by William Gates between 1777 and 1783 is in marked contrast to that of Bradburn, being veneered in the then-fashionable light-coloured satinwood and inlaid instead of being carved. In 1781

---

[1] H. Clifford Smith, o p. cit., page 90.

Below, *Fig. 88: Inlaid mahogany dressing table. Circa 1795; width closed 88·9 cm. (Private collection.)*

Right, *Plate 14: Inlaid satinwood Pembroke table. Circa 1780; top open, 81·3 cm. square. (In the Saloon, Saltram, Devon: The National Trust.)*

he supplied a pair of half-round commodes for the apartments of the Prince of Wales in the Queen's House, two years prior to his removal to Carlton House. Both the actual pieces of furniture and the invoice for them survive, and the commodes show Gates to have been a very skilled worker in inlaying neo-classical motifs.

Many other makers of about the same date were supplying pieces with similar ornamentation, and the Pembroke table in Plate 14, of satinwood inlaid with other woods of contrasting colours, is an outstanding example. The Pembroke, with its convenient hinged flaps, acquired its name at some time in the second half of the 18th Century. In 1803 Thomas Sheraton called it 'a kind of breakfast table, from the name of the lady who first gave orders for one of them'. The lady in question remains anonymous, but a more modern suggestion is that the ninth Earl of Pembroke, who had an interest in architecture and design and died in 1750, is more likely to have brought it into being.

Of a much rarer type than the preceding table is that shown in Plate 15 and Fig. 90. The top is of the so-called 'envelope' type, and because it has been kept closed for most of its life the colours of the interior are almost as they were when new. The squares are of harewood, the name given to sycamore which has been stained to a light brown-grey colour.

Below, *Fig. 89: The dressing table in Fig. 88 with the top opened. (Private collection.)*

8 : Irish Cabinet-Making

WHILE some Irish manufactures, notably cut glass, cannot usually be differentiated from those of England, this is not the case with furniture. Although close geographically and allied politically, in artistic matters the countries were less often in conformity. With furniture not only was the overall appearance distinctive, but the choice of ornament and the style of rendering it was equally individual.

A visitor to the country in the early 17th Century, the traveller, Fynes Moryson, wrote scathingly of the Irish country-folk who, he said,

> . . . have no tables, but set meat upon a bundle of grass, and use the same grass as napkins to wipe their hands . . . I trust no man expects among these gallants any beds, much less feather beds and sheets. . . .

Of the sophisticated places he added: 'In cities passengers may have feather beds soft and good, but most uncommonly lousy'; which was a state of affairs paralleled everywhere else at that date and considerably later.

Some of the more important mansions of the time differed little in their contents from English ones, with inventories which detail tapestries, chairs, stools, beds and brilliantly-coloured fabrics.[1] Apart from such written evidence, little or nothing has survived the centuries of strife that have beset the country from the earliest times and continue into the present.

With the advent of the 18th Century the picture becomes clearer, and there is a variety of surviving furniture increasing in quantity as the century progresses. Again, there is in some instances a likeness to English homes. On her first visit to Dublin, in October 1731, the observant Mary Pendarves made no reference to visible differences between house-furnishing in that city and London. She was at the house of Dr. Clayton, Bishop of Killala, and

---

[1] The Knight of Glin (Desmond Fitz-Gerald), 'Some Inventories and Irish Furniture', in *A Guide to Irish Antiques*, ed. G. Stacpoole, Cork, 1969.

Left, *Plate 15: Table on a carved tripod base, the folding 'envelope' top inlaid with harewood (sycamore), holly and other woods.* Circa *1785; top 68 cm. square.* (Private collection.)

recorded in a letter to her sister:

> First there is a very good hall well filled with servants, then a room of eighteen foot square, wainscoted with oak, the panels all carved, and the doors and chimney finished with very fine high carving, the ceiling stucco, the window-curtains and chairs yellow Genoa damask, portraits and landscapes, very well done, round the room, marble [topped] tables between the windows, and looking-glasses with gilt frames. The next room is twenty-eight foot long and twenty-two broad, and is as finely adorned as damask, pictures, and busts can make it, besides the floor being entirely covered with the finest Persian carpet that ever was seen. The bed-chamber is large and handsome, all furnished with the same damask.[1]

Despite the fact that examples of 18th-Century Irish furniture are extant, much research remains to be carried out in order to bring to light the names of the designers, makers and suppliers who are at present unknown. Until recently the very existence of true Irish furniture has often been deliberately ignored, and specimens have been dubbed 'English' to increase their value and make them saleable. This approach is less common than it once was, and the productions of Irish workshops are now more widely recognised as possessing a manifest and admirable individuality.

Most Irish furniture takes the form of versions of English prototypes, but a notable exception exists in a set of walnut and marquetry chairs which are quite plainly of Dutch inspiration. They have elaborately curved outlines to the backs and seats, the cabriole legs are carved with shells on the knees, and the feet are two-tiered with scrolls above weak versions of the claw-and-ball. Their origin is attested by the

signature on one of them, which reads: 'Maher Kilkenny 1740 Fecit'.[2]

The majority of the furniture is made of mahogany and has in the past usually been termed erroneously 'Irish-Chippendale', probably in the main because of the timber from which it is constructed. In fact, many surviving examples pre-date the *Director*, and the majority show only a moderate use of Rococo motifs with little trace of the lightness and movement associated with the style in England and elsewhere.

The furniture is characterised by a solidity of appearance and a stiffness of line, as well as by some other features that are peculiar to it alone. In particular the Irish craftsmen favoured carving, but carving that is noticeably much flatter than that of their English counterparts. A variety of motifs was employed, but they were often rendered in a manner that bordered on the grotesque and which lends the finished work a provincial air.

The heaviness of many pieces, especially those for use in dining rooms, has been remarked upon and perhaps reflects the extravagant eating habits of those who used them. Writing in 1752, referring to a meal at the home of Dr. Synge, Bishop of Elphin, Mrs. Delany wrote.

> We had a magnificent dinner, extremely well drest and well attended . . . The Bishop lives constantly very well, and it becomes his station and fortune, but *high living is too much the fashion here.* You are not invited to dinner to any private gentleman of a £1000 a year or

---

[1] Mrs. Pendarves was born Mary Granville, after the death of Alexander Pendarves in 1724 she later married Patrick Delany, Dean of Down. The quotation is from *The Autobiography and Correspondence of Mary Granville, Mrs. Delany,* ed. Lady Llanover, 6 vols., 1861–2, vol. I, page 305.

[2] Illustrated in Anthony Coleridge and The Knight of Glin, 'Eighteenth Century Irish Furniture', in *Apollo,* October 1966, page 276.

less, that does not give you seven *dishes* at one course, and Burgundy and Champagne; and these dinners they give once or twice a-week, that provision is now as dear as in London. I own I am surprised *how* they manage; for we cannot afford anything like it, with a *much better* income than most of those who give these entertainments.[1]

HABITS had changed a couple of decades later when Richard Twiss visited the island in 1775. He spent 43 hours sailing to

Dublin from Aberystwyth, and noted:

I landed in Ireland with an opinion that the inhabitants were addicted to drinking, given to hospitality, and apt to blunder, or make bulls; in which I found myself mistaken. Hospitality and drinking went formerly hand in hand, but since the excesses of the table have been so judiciously abolished, hospitality is not so violently practised

---

[1] Op. cit., vol. III, page 87.

Left, *Fig. 90: Table with inlaid folding top and carved mahogany tripod base, see Plate 15 for a view of the table with the top open.*

Below, *Fig. 91: Irish mahogany table on cabriole supports, the apron centring on an eagle. Mid-18th Century; width 91.5 cm. (Christies.)*

as heretofore, when it might have been imputed to them as a fault.[1]

Typical of pieces made in the first half of the 18th Century are the tables illustrated in Figs. 91, 92 and 93. All date from *c*. 1740–1750, and share characteristically-shaped cabriole legs with only a slight curve to them, which suggests an economy in the use of wood as much as any lack of skill on the part of designer or maker. Each, too, has a hairy claw-and-ball foot, above which is an excrescence, in one instance a leaf and in the other what is apparently a curl of hair. The stool in Fig. 95 has similar terminations to the legs and is likewise flatly carved on the knees and apron.

In some tables the design centres on the head of an animal, presumably that of a lion but more often closer in resemblance to a Pekinese puppy (Fig. 94). Surfaces forming the background to relief carving were

---

[1] Richard Twiss, *A Tour in Ireland in 1775*, 1776.

Below, *Fig. 92: Table of similar type to that in Fig. 91, but the apron centred on a shell. Mid-18th Century; width 120·7 cm. (Private collection.)*

frequently incised with diaper patterns or punched. While shallow cross-hatching was employed to give variety, as on the ribs of the scallop shell on the apron of the stool in Fig. 95. While some of the tables were fitted with wooden tops, others were surmounted by slabs of marble of local origin.

A further feature of many 18th-Century Irish houses was a profusion of buckets made of mahogany hooped with bands of brass. They were used for holding supplies of peat for the fires, or for carrying plates to and from dining rooms and kitchens. For the latter purpose they were constructed with a slit down the front, so that the contents could be handled with ease during filling and emptying. Most were fitted with a hinged bail handle as in Fig. 96 but the more decorative example in Fig. 97 is ribbed horizontally and has small oval handles at each side. Large numbers of such articles have been imported into England and other countries during the past two centuries and many identical ones were made elsewhere than in Ireland, so it is no longer possible to be certain as to where the majority originated.

Below, *Fig. 93: Table of similar type to those in Figs. 91 and 92, the apron carved with exotic birds, flowers and fruit and with a male mask. Mid-18th Century; width about 150 cm. (Private collection.)*

On the other hand, the frame of the look-ing-glass in Fig. 99 could have emanated from nowhere else but an Irish workshop. It exhibits almost every element of the native repertoire: the overall flat carving, the use of incised diaper as a background, and the stiff drawing. This last is especially noticeable in the eagle at the top and the two birds below, which may or may not have been intended to have been all of the same breed. The use of mahogany throughout is also distinctive; in an English frame the mahogany would undoubtedly have been relieved by an inner slip of gilt wood, plain

or carved. In contrast to the unreality of the birds it may be noticed that the scrolls on which they rest are carved with a fluidity of line that would not disgrace a London craftsman.

It is known that Thomas Chippendale's *Director* was available in Dublin, for the title-page of the first (1754) edition an-nounced that copies could be obtained there, where they were sold 'by Mr. John Smith, on the Blind Quay'. How many were dis-posed of by him is not known and probably never will be, but the Irish designers and cabinet-makers would seem to have done no

Left, *Fig. 94: Irish mahogany card table, the apron centred on a lion mask. Mid-18th Century; width 91·5 cm. (Sotheby's.)*

Below, *Fig. 95: Irish mahogany stool, the apron flatly carved and centred on a shell, and the cabriole legs terminating in lions' paw feet below a leafy scroll. Mid-18th Century; width 78·7 cm. (Christie's.)*

more than glance briefly at the contents of the book. It had slight or no obvious effect on their output.

Little English furniture was apparently brought into Ireland in the first three-quarters of the 18th Century. There is evidence, indeed, that some of the wealthier residents made purchases in London from time to time. Peter Langlois, William and John Linnell and the firm of Gillows are among those who are known to have supplied such clients, but they were exceptions.

Below, Fig. 96: Brass-bound mahogany bucket probably of Irish make. Late 18th Century; height 39 cm. (Private collection.)

Right, Fig. 97: Straight-sided bucket of mahogany hooped with brass and with handles at opposite sides. Late 18th Century; height 46 cm. (Private collection.)

Throughout the century the London Parliament would not permit the Irish to export any of their manufactures, while those of England might be sent across the Irish Sea to gain what profit they could in the small and captive nearby market. In retaliation, the Dubliners did their utmost to present a solid front in favour of non-importation, and their own manufacturers were forced to struggle along by supplying only buyers in their own country.

THE outbreak of the War of Independence in America in 1775 led to a change. The English became alarmed lest the French, who favoured the Americans, should attempt to attack England by way of Ireland. So the Dublin Parliament was called on to raise a defence force, and before long some 40,000 men had responded to the call. Although they were normally divided in their loyalties, for once they became united under the leadership of the eloquent statesman, Henry Grattan. He argued strenuously and irresistibly in favour of freedom to trade where and with whom they pleased, and faced with the possibility that the 40,000 might desert their cause London had little option but to concede the point in 1780.

The best-known result of the newly won trading privilege was the establishing of a number of glass-houses by joint Anglo-Irish enterprise, of which that at Waterford remains a household word. Glass was heavily taxed in England, so there was an obvious advantage to be gained by making it in a country where no such impediment existed. Furniture was not subject to the disability, and therefore did not present the same inducement to cabinet-makers. Nonetheless, at least one cabinet-maker made the crossing, and judging by his surname he may well have been returning to his homeland. The date when he did so may have been merely a coincidence and have had no connection with other events. However, he advertised his presence in the capital by the

following announcement in the pages of the *Dublin Evening Post* during May 1782:

> William Moore most respectfully acknowledges the encouragement he has received, begs leave to inform those who may want Inlaid work, that by his close attention to business and instructions to his men, he has brought the manufacture to such perfection, to be able to sell for almost one half his original prices; as the greatest demand is for Pier-Tables, he has just finished in the newest taste a great variety of patterns, sizes and prices, from three guineas to twenty; Card tables on a new construction (both ornamented and plain) which appear like small Pier Tables, with every article in the inlaid Way, executed on shortest notice, and hopes from his long experience at Messrs. Mayhew & Ince, London, his remarkable fine coloured woods, and elegant finished work, to meet the approbation of all who shall be pleased to honour him with their commands.

Below, *Fig. 98: Commode ornamented with marquetry in various woods on a ground of harewood, by William Moore, Dublin. Circa 1785; width 141·6 cm. (Victoria and Albert Museum.)*

Right, *Fig. 99: Looking-glass in a carved mahogany frame showing characteristic features of Irish cabinet-making. Mid-18th Century. (Private collection.)*

The precise date of Moore's arrival in Ireland is not recorded, but his first Dublin address was in Abbey Street. In 1791 he moved to Capel Street, and from soon after that date he described himself as 'Cabinet and Pianoforte Maker'. Just prior to the appearance of his advertisement the third Duke of Portland reached Dublin to take up his appointment as Viceroy, and a commode supplied to him by Moore is now at Welbeck Abbey in the possession of the Duke's descendants.

Below, Fig. 100: Secretaire-cabinet decorated with marquetry of neo-classical pattern and perhaps of Irish make. Circa 1785; width 124·5 cm. (Parke-Bernet Galleries, Inc.)

Right, Plate 16: Armchair and gout stool of satinwood inlaid with ebony stringing, supplied by Thomas Chippendale the Younger in 1802. (Stourhead, Wiltshire: The National Trust.)

Another commode, now in the Victoria and Albert Museum (Fig. 98), is attributed to William Moore because of its similarity to the Portland example and to a pair once at Lismore, County Waterford. The commode is inlaid in coloured woods on a harewood ground with a pattern of scrolls, garlands of husks, and vases, and on the front is a central oval panel with roses and buds. Distinctive features are the vases which are noticeably tall and thin, and the general delicacy and grace of the design.

The shape of the vases on the foregoing piece may be compared with those on the secretaire in Fig. 100. It is altogether of most elaborate design, with serpentine front and sides, the former descending to a simple concave curve, and with a hooded superstructure centred on a shaped bank of six small drawers. The lower part is fitted with drawers, of which the topmost one has a hinged front concealing the secretaire.

One of Moore's pianos is little less unorthodox in appearance than the latter piece of furniture. It is semi-circular in shape, raised on square tapering legs and when closed might easily be mistaken for a pier table.[1] Whether the unusual form affected the tone of the instrument is not recorded.

A worthwhile subject for careful investigation, Mr. Desmond Fitz-Gerald has written: 'The study of Irish furniture is still in its infancy, for so little documentation exists during the early and mid-18th Century. For example, I know of no 18th-Century pieces accompanied by their bills or cabinet-maker's name. The newspapers frequently carried advertisements for oak, walnut, japanned and gilt furniture, but it is all but impossible to link them with recognised pieces'.[2] It is to be hoped that work now in progress will bear fruit, and in the future Irish furniture will be at least no less well documented than English.

---

[1] Illustrated in Clifford Musgrave, *Adam and Hepplewhite and Other Neo-classical Furniture*, 1966, Fig. 170.

[2] The Knight of Glin, op. cit., page 56.

9 : Thomas Shearer &
The Firm of Seddon

THOMAS Shearer is another of the sha-
dowy figures connected with 18th-Cen-
tury cabinet-making. No details of his life
and career, no labelled furniture, bills or
other written documents have survived.
Although he is often described as having
been a cabinet-maker, there is at present no
proof that this was so and he may have been
a skilled draughtsman rather than an arti-
ficer. His claim to remembrance is that he
was responsible for the majority of the
drawings engraved in a volume entitled:

> The Cabinet-Maker's London Book of
> Prices, and Designs of Cabinet Work,
> calculated for the Convenience of
> Cabinet Makers in General: Whereby
> the Price of executing any Piece of
> Work may be easily found.

It was first issued in 1788, and further,
amended, editions appeared in 1793, 1805
and 1823.

The drawings not by Shearer are signed
'Hepplewhite del.', presumably because
they were the work of George Hepplewhite.
The latter died in 1786, the *Guide* bearing
his name being published by his widow two
years later. It may be noted that the
Hepplewhite drawings in the Shearer book
are dated 1792, the year when they were
engraved for the second edition, so it may be
wondered whether his widow did not get
someone else to execute them and put her
surname to them. At any rate, there remains a mystery concerning them which
perhaps time will solve.

The book mainly comprises lists of prices
for various operations in making the pieces

Below, *Fig. 101: Designs for drawer
fitments, by Thomas Shearer, 1788.*

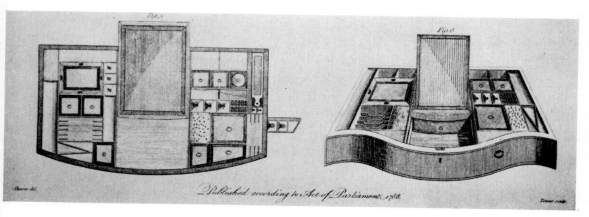

illustrated in the plates. They are of interest in showing the numerous refinements in finish and construction that might be applied, such as extra mouldings, veneering and so forth. Thus, the dressing table illustrating Fig. 102 is detailed, in part, as follows:

	£	s.	d.
A Harlequin Table Two feet two inches long, one foot nine inches from back to front, three feet high, folding tops and taper'd legs, a writing flap in the top, square clamp'd, with a horse [adjustable rest] under ditto, the harlequin to rise with springs, seven drawers and four letter holes inside, one drawer and and one sham ditto in front, cock beaded, a cupboard below with hollow tambour to run right and left, and an astragal on the edge of the bottom.	3	6	0
Extras.			
Each inch, more or less, in length or width	0	0	9
Making the harlequin to rise with weights	0	2	6

Casting the weights . .	0	0	9
Making the above round front, extra	0	7	0
Ditto serpentine . . .	0	10	0
Extra drawer in a straight front	0	2	6
Ditto in a round front . .	0	3	3
Ditto in a serpentine . .	0	3	9
Veneering straight front, when one drawer . . .	0	1	3
Ditto each extra drawer .	0	0	6
Veneering round front, when one drawer	0	1	6
Ditto each extra drawer .	0	0	7
Veneering serpentine front, when one drawer . . .	0	2	0
Each extra drawer . .	0	0	9
A pair of door frames for wire work in place of tambour .	0	3	0
Veneering door frames long-way	0	2	0
Ditto cross-way . . .	0	3	0
Oiling and polishing . .	0	1	0

The plates show a variety of pieces of furniture, of which the most novel at the time is a sideboard constructed in one piece, in place of the earlier use of a table flanked by separate pedestals (see Fig. 63, page 83). The writing table with a low curving super-structure, known at a later date as a Carlton House Table, appears as 'A Gentle-man's Writing Table', and there is one plate devoted to details of the interior fittings of the drawers of dressing chests and secretaires (Fig. 101).

Below, *Fig. 103: Mahogany serpentine-fronted sideboard on moulded legs. Circa 1790; width 148 cm. (Private collection.)*

Two little-known engravers executed the plates, which are signed either 'Towes' or 'H. Elbon, 21 St. Martin's le Grand'. According to the title-page the book was published by The London Society of Cabinet-Makers, and was for sale at three addresses in London. None of them was that of a bookseller, but each was a public house; *The White Swan*, Shoe Lane, *The Marquis of Granby*, Castle Street, Oxford Market, and *The Unicorn*, Henrietta Street, Covent Garden. This surely indicates that the book was intended for the use of practising master-craftsmen, and that the latter perhaps constituted a regularly organised body.

Some years earlier there were signs that discontent was rife among the work-people in the trade, and that some kind of alliance for self-protection existed in spite of such groupings being illegal. In November 1761 a notice was printed in the *London Gazette*, which was duly summarised in the *Gentleman's Magazine* (Vol. XXXI, page 532):

> Saturday 7 [November]. An order of council was issued, to suppress the unlawful combination of the journeymen-cabinet makers, and to enjoin all magistrates to prosecute the masters of public-houses, where such journeymen shall resort.

Below, *Fig. 104: Design for a sideboard by Thomas Shearer, published in* The Cabinet-Makers' London Book of Prices, *1788.*

This was followed by an advertisement in the pages of the *General Evening Post* of 21–24 November 1761 (No. 4386):

At a Meeting of the Master Cabinet and Chair-makers at the Crown and Anchor Tavern in the Strand, Nov. 18, 1761, it was unanimously resolved, That all Journeymen Cabinet and Chair-makers who are willing to return to work, on the usual Terms of those Trades, shall meet with all Encouragement due to their Merit from the Masters in general, without signing any Article whatever; such Signing being only proposed to discover such as were misled by a too hasty Compliance with the Advice of a few inconsiderate Men. And those who do not return to work, will be considered by the Masters as Persons bidding Defiance to the Order of the Lords of his Majesty's most Honourable Privy-Council, and must blame themselves for the Consequences.[1]

The event duly proved infectious, not unexpectedly in the days when Wilkes was earning the plaudits of the mob, and a year later Horace Walpole referred to similar troubles in a letter to Sir Horace Mann:

I am in distress about my gallery and cabinet [at Strawberry Hill]: the latter was on the point of being completed, and is really striking beyond description. Last Saturday night [25 June] my workmen took their leave, made their bow, and left me up to the knees in shavings. In short, the journeymen carpenters, like the cabinet-makers, have entered into an association not to work unless their wages are raised; and how can one complain? The poor fellows, whose all their labour is, see their masters advance their prices every day, and think it reasonable to touch their share.[2]

It was a long-enduring affair, for a month later the carpenters were still not working. A sentence in a letter written by the same

Below, Fig. 105: Satinwood and mahogany secretaire-cabinet, the clock inscribed 'Week's Museum' probably made by Seddons. Circa 1795; width 96.5 cm. (Parke-Bernet Galleries, Inc.) **Right,** *Fig. 106: Satinwood Pembroke table painted with lily-of-the-valley, roses and other flowers, ensuite with the card table in Fig. 107 and supplied by Seddon, Sons & Shackleton in 1793. Width open 99.5 cm. (Private collection.)*

[1] The Crown and Anchor was widely patronised, Johnson and Boswell dined there, and the house boasted a room measuring 84 ft. by 35 ft. 6 in. in which a banquet for 2,000 people was given in 1798. The building was burnt down in 1854.

[2] 1 July 1762. Op. cit., Vol. V, page 219. It is pertinent at the present day to quote the next sentence in the above letter: 'You would be frightened at the dearness of everything; I build out of economy, for unless I do now, in two years I shall not be able to afford it.'

correspondent to the Earl of Strafford on 5 August mentioned the matter again:

> Your château [Wentworth Castle, Yorkshire], I hope, proceeds faster than mine. The carpenters are all associated for increase of wages; I have had but two men at work these five weeks.[1]

THE firm of Seddon is emerging as one of the more important London cabinet-makers active during the last quarter of the 18th Century, and later. The founder was George Seddon, who was born in Lancashire in 1727 and apprenticed in London at the age of 16. He duly took premises in Aldersgate Street, in the City of London, which were known as London House and had for some time been the residence of the Bishops of London. From an entry in a directory published in 1763 it is known that Seddon was then at that address, and five

years later it was damaged by fire. The occurrence was reported in identical words in both the *Annual Register* (Vol. XI, page [139]) and the *Gentleman's Magazine* (Vol. XXXVIII, page 347):

> Thursday [July] 14. A dreadful fire burnt down London House, formerly the residence of the bishops of London, in Aldersgate-street, now occupied by Mr. Seddon, one of the most eminent cabinet-makers in London. The damage is computed at £20,000.

Re-building took place, but in 1783 another fire, far bigger than the earlier one, broke out. This time it was on 5th November, anniversary of the Gunpowder Plot, and a not improbable date for a confla-

---

[1] Ibid., page 229.

Below, *Fig. 107: Pair of card tables matching the Pembroke table in Fig. 106, and supplied by Seddons in 1793. Width of each 99·5 cm. (Private collection.)*

Right, *Fig. 108: Giltwood tripod candelabrum supplied by Seddons in 1793. One of a pair for which £21 was charged, see Fig. 109. Height 172·5 cm. (Private collection.)*

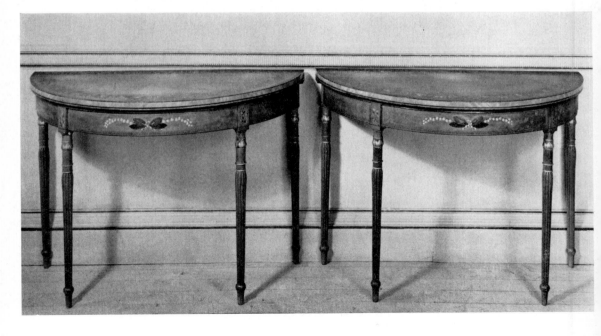

gration. The *Gentleman's Magazine* (Vol. LIII, page 974) reported it at some length:

> About a quarter after one in the morning a most alarming fire broke out in the workshops behind Mr. Seddon's dwelling-house in Aldersgate Street. They were full of cabinet work, of the choicest workmanship, with great quantities of rough mahogany, unwrought, which were almost instantly in a blaze, and illuminated the streets to a great distance. The cabinet-work burnt so fiercely that there was no possibility of stopping the progress of the flames, till the whole, together with more than 50 adjoining houses, were either burnt, or so much damaged as to be rendered uninhabitable for some time. The scene of distress, occasioned by this accident, was truly pitiable. The whole loss is computed at more than £100,000, the principal part of which must fall on the Fire-Offices.—Mr. Seddon's house, some years ago, was burnt down, just as, by some neglect, its policy of insurance had been suffered to run out, by which he lost his All.

In fact, although he had not paid his insurance premium in time in 1768 the Sun Insurance Office, with which he was insured for £3,300, allowed him 'in Consideration of his great Distress' the sum of £500.[1]

George, the younger son of George Seddon, joined the firm in 1785 or 1786, and in the latter year the premises were visited by a German novelist, Sophie von la Roche. She has left a description of what she saw, although it is plain that here and there she was either misinformed or making bad guesses. Thus, her mention that 'In the basement mirrors are cast and cut' is certainly inaccurate. Seddons bill-heads proclaim them to be 'Manufacturers of British Cast Large Plate Glass' (Fig. 110), but they

[1] G. Bernard Hughes, 'George Seddon of London House' in *Apollo*, May 1957.

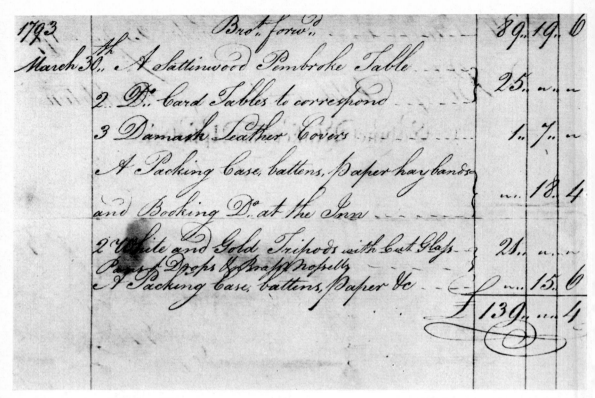

could not possibly have carried this out in the City. More probably it was a form of words to convey a financial interest in, or merely an agency for, the British Cast Plate Glass Manufacturers, of Ravenhead, St. Helens, Lancashire, which was established in 1773 to make glass by the method of casting practised with success for a century by the French.

Sophie von la Roche remarked enthusiastically on the many different articles for sale, which were 'in all manner of woods and patterns, from the simplest and cheapest to the most elegant and expensive'.[1] She was particularly attracted by a sideboard with matching pedestals at each end, the latter surmounted by vases to hold knives, forks and spoons, which was 'extremely tasteful in ornamenting a dining-room'. She also noted:

> Numerous articles made of straw-coloured service wood and charmingly finished with all the cabinet-maker's skill.[2] Chintz, silk and wool materials for curtains and bed-covers; hangings of every possible material; carpets and stair-carpets to order; in short, anything one might desire to furnish a house; and all the workmen besides and a great many seamstresses . . .

[1] *Sophie in London, 1786,* trans. by Clare Williams, 1933, pages 173–5.

[2] Service wood: presumably this is satinwood.

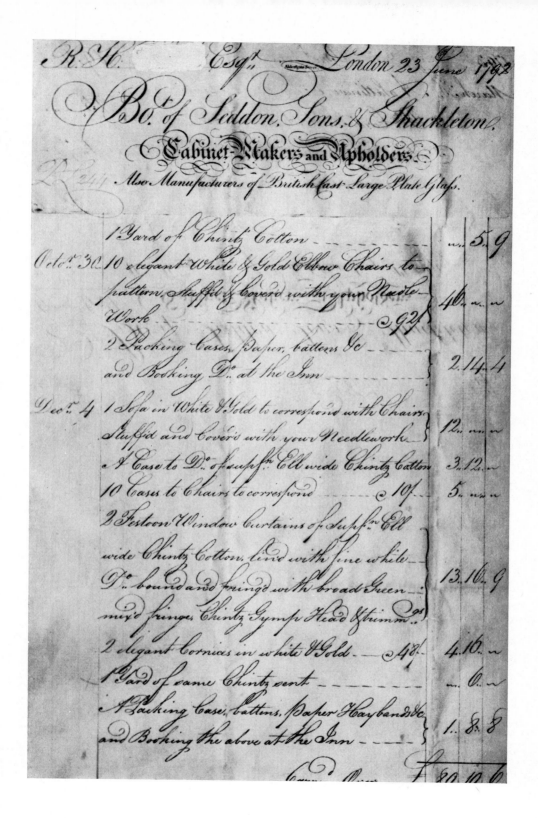

R.H. ————— Esqr ————— London 23 June 1792

Bo^t of Seddon, Sons, & Shackleton,
Cabinet Makers and Upholders
Also Manufacturers of British Cast Large Plate Glass.

	1 Yard of Chintz Cotton ————————		5	9
Octo^r 30	10 elegant White & Gold Elbow Chairs to pattern, Stuff'd & Cover'd with your Needle Work ———— 92/		46	
	2 Packing Cases, Paper, battens &c and Booking D^o at the Inn ————————		2.14.4
Decr 4	1 Sofa in White & Gold to correspond with Chairs Stuff'd and Cover'd with your Needlework		12	
	A Case to D^o of sup^{fn} Ell wide Chintz Cotton		3.12	
	10 Cases to Chairs to correspond ———— 10/		5	
	2 Festoon Window Curtains of Sup^{fn} Ell wide Chintz Cotton, lined with fine white D^o bound and fring'd with broad Green mix'd fringe, Chintz Gymp Head &trimm^g		13.16.9
	2 elegant Cornices in white & Gold —— 48/		4.16	
	1 Yard of same Chintz sent ————————		6	
	A Packing Case, battens, Paper Haybands &c and Booking the above at the Inn —————		1. 8. 8
	Carr^d Over ————— £ 80.19.6			

Below, *Fig. 111: Inlaid satinwood secretaire-cabinet. Circa 1780; width 100 cm. (John Keil, Ltd.)*

Right, *Fig. 112: The same secretaire-cabinet closed. It has been attributed to Seddons.*

By 1790 the firm included George Seddon's elder son, Thomas, and his son-in-law, Thomas Shackleton, thenceforward being styled 'Seddon, Sons and Shackleton'. The founder died in 1801, when the *Gentleman's Magazine* (Vol. LXXXI, part ii, page 1152) briefly noted his passing:

> [December] 26. At his house at Hampstead, George Seddon, esq. of Aldersgate-street.

Members of the family continued the business into the 19th Century. A very small proportion of the output, which must have been considerable in quantity, has been found to bear printed labels. A sofa table has been recorded with the impressed stamp 'T & G Seddon', but all the marked examples so far noted date to about the year 1820.

A suite of a Pembroke table and a pair of semi-circular card tables in painted satinwood is illustrated in Figs. 106 and 107, together with the original bill for supplying them in 1792 (Figs. 109 and 110). The three pieces cost a total of £25, plus 27s. for '3 Damask Leather Covers' and 18s. 4d. for packing materials, etc. On the same bill is a pair of candelabra, of giltwood with metal and glass fittings, which cost £21 (Fig. 108). A set of ten armchairs and a settee was also part of the same purchase, and was described as follows:

10 elegant White & Gold Elbow Chairs to pattern, Stuff'd & Cover'd with your Needlework @ 92/-	46	—	—
2 Packing Cases, paper, battens, &c. and BookingD°. at the Inn	2	14	4
1 Sofa in White & Gold to correspond with Chairs Stuff'd & Cover'd with your Needlework	12	—	—
A Case of D°. of sup^{fn}. Ell wide Chintz Cotton	3	12	0
10 Cases to Chairs to correspond @ 10/-	5	—	—

Regrettably, these were sold some years before the discovery of Seddons' bill, and as no illustrations of them exist it is very unlikely that they will ever be identified.

The late 18th-Century productions that have so far been identified are of excellent

Below, *Fig. 113: Satinwood secretaire-cabinet with painted decoration, perhaps made by Seddons. Circa 1790; width 84·5 cm. (Arlington Court, Devon: The National Trust.)*

Right, *Plate 18: Figured mahogany breakfront wardrobe, one of the drawer tops showing traces of a stamp having been obliterated. Probably made by Gillows of Lancaster. Circa 1800; width 191 cm. (Private collection.)*

workmanship, but reveal no outstanding features in their design. On the whole, outlines and details follow those popularised by Hepplewhite and Shearer, with nothing by which to differentiate them from the work of the numerous other makers active at the same date. Nothing has yet been attributed to the elder George Seddon's earlier years, so what he made between about 1750 and 1780 remains unidentified.

It has been thought probable that Seddons were responsible for a number of satinwood secretaire-cabinets, some of which have a shaped pediment centred on a clock. In at least two instances the clock is inscribed 'Weeks's Museum', as in the specimen in Fig. 105. The Museum was a collection of mechanical and other curiosities on view to the public in 'Tichborne Street', London,[1] of which 'the Grand Room, by Wyatt, had a ceiling painted by Rebecca and Singleton'. Presumably the cabinets were shown there,

and sold, amid the automata, 'clocks and candelabra, miniatures, musical birdboxes, watches, etc.'.

One other of the firm's achievements deserves a mention: in 1814 they were responsible for making a cradle, now in the Peel Park Museum, Salford, intended for the reception of the 'Prince of Peace'. The birth of the child had been prophesised by the Devonshire-born religious fanatic, Joanna Southcott, who was then over sixty years of age, and she announced that it would take place on 19th October 1814. When the day arrived the disappointed world was told that Joanna was in a trance, and in the following December she died of brain fever.

---

[1] John Timbs, *Curiosities of London*, 1868. Some bracket clocks are known with the address Coventry Street.

10 : Thomas Sheraton

MOST of the basic information about Thomas Sheraton's life and career is contained in an obituary printed in the *Gentleman's Magazine* in 1806 (Vol. LXXVI, part ii, page 1082), which reads:

> [October] 22. In Broad-street, Soho, after a few days illness of a phrenitis, aged 55, Mr. Thomas Sheraton, a native of Stockton-upon-Tees, and for many years a journeyman cabinet-maker, but who, since about the year 1793, has supported himself, a wife, and two children, by his exertions as an author. In 1793 he published a work, in 2 volumes, 4to, intituled 'The Cabinetmaker and Upholsterer's Drawing-book', to which is prefixed a numerous list of subscribers, including almost all the principal cabinet-makers in town and country. Since that time he has published 30 numbers, in folio, of a work intended to be completed in 125 numbers, intituled 'The Cabinet-maker and Artist's Encyclopaedia', of which he sold nearly a thousand copies. In order to increase the number of his subscribers to this work, he had lately visited Ireland, where he obtained the sanction of the Lord Lieutenant, the Marchioness of Donegal, and other distinguished persons. He was a very honest, well-disposed man; of an acute and enterprising disposition; but, like many other self-taught authors, shewed the want of a regular education in his writings. He has left his family, it is feared, in distressed circumstances.

There is no reason to doubt that Sheraton spent some of his years working as a cabinet-maker. None of his productions have been identified, and it is perhaps likely that he was an employee rather than in business on his own account. His trade-card, on which the side of a room with windows, chairs and a large column are flanked by drawing instruments and a copy of his *Drawing Book*, announces:

> T. Sheraton, N°. 106, Wardour Street, Soho—Teaches Perspective, Architecture and Ornaments, makes designs for Cabinet-makers, and sells all kinds of Drawing Books Etc.[1]

In 1793, according to the title-page of the *Drawing-Book*, he was living at 41 Davies Street, Grosvenor Square, but soon afterwards he had moved to Wardour Street.

In addition to his activities as a cabinet-maker and a draughtsman, he wrote some religious tracts and in 1782, while he was still at Stockton, published *A Scriptural Illustration of the Doctrine of Regeneration* and *A Letter on the Subject of Baptism*. Later, in 1805, he published *A Discourse on the Character of God as Love*, and he was said to have preached sporadically in Baptist pulpits.

The Scottish publisher, Adam Black, came to London when a young man to learn

---

[1] Ambrose Heal, op. cit., page 167.

the bookselling trade, and in 1804 he lodged for a week in Sheraton's house. He left a record of the impressions he gained of his landlord and family which confirms the information in the obituary and adds some details. 'Sheraton', he wrote,

> lived in a poor street in London, his house half shop, half dwelling-house, and himself looked like a worn-out Methodist minister, with threadbare black coat. I took tea with them one afternoon. There was a cup and saucer for the host, and another for his wife,

and a little porringer for their daughter. The wife's cup and saucer were given to me. and she had to put up with another little porringer. My host seemed a good man, with some talent. He had been a cabinet-maker, and was now author, publisher, and teacher of drawing, and, I believe occasional preacher.

Black summed him up in these words:

> This many-sided worn-out encyclopaedist and preacher is an interesting character. . . . He is a man of talent and, I believe, of genuine piety. He under-

Left, *Plate 19: Cupboard of mahogany inset with coloured marbles in the front and top, the latter with a turned gallery. Circa 1800; width 49 cm. (Private collection.)*

Below, *Fig. 113: Designs for chair backs by Thomas Sheraton, 1792.*

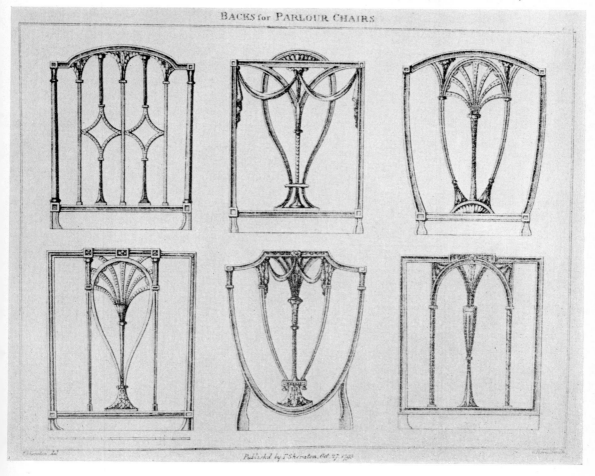

Above, *Fig. 114: Satinwood Cylinder Desk and Bookcase, after a design in Thomas Sheraton's* Cabinet-Maker and Upholsterer's Drawing-Book, *1792. Circa 1790: width about 76 cm. (John Keil, Ltd.)*

Right, *Fig. 115: Inlaid mahogany 'Lady's Writing Table', after a design in Sheraton's Drawing-Book dated 1792. Circa 1790; width about 76 cm. (Mallett & Son, Ltd.)*

stands the cabinet business—and I believe was bred to it. He is a scholar, writes well, and, in my opinion, draws masterly—is an author, bookseller, stationer and teacher. . . . I believe his abilities and resources are his ruin in this respect—by attempting to do everything he does nothing.[1]

Thomas Sheraton's principal contribution to the history of English furniture is his first publication, *The Cabinet-Maker and Upholsterer's Drawing-Book*, which was first issued in 1793–4, was re-issued with some additional plates in the latter year, and reached a third edition in 1803. The plates are dated variously between 1791 and 1794, and were the work of several engravers who illustrated books of various types.

The volume opens with an address 'to Cabinet-makers and upholsterers in General', in the course of which the author critically surveys the work of his predecessors. He examines their draughtsmanship with regard to what it might teach the reader, and finds them all lacking in that respect as well as being out-dated. None is spared, and he opens with a withering blast:

> I have seen one book of designs which seems to have been published before Chippendale's. I infer this from the antique appearance of the furniture, for there is no date to it; but the title informs us that it was composed by a Society of Cabinet-makers in London. It gives no instructions for drawing in any form, but we may venture to say that those who drew the designs wanted a good share of teaching themselves.[2]

Robert Manwaring and Ince and Mayhew are the next to be castigated; the latter's book 'may be said to have been a book of merit in its day, though much inferior to Chippendale's, which was a real original, as well as more extensive and masterly in its designs'. Chippendale, however, was not allowed to escape without his share of censure. His designs, Sheraton wrote, 'are now wholly antiquated and laid aside, though possessed of great merit, according to the times in which they were executed'. Some of Hepplewhite's drawings, he admits, 'are not without merit, though it is evident that the perspective is, in some instances, erroneous'. Convinced that the

[1] *Memoirs of Adam Black*, ed. Alexander Nicholson, 2nd edition, Edinburgh, 1885.

[2] Sheraton must have seen a copy of the undated second edition of *Genteel Household Furniture* which, in fact, came out at least six years after Chippendale's *Director*.

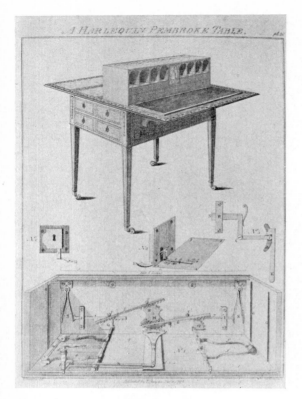

A HARLEQUIN PEMBROKE TABLE.

Above, *Fig. 116: Sheraton's design for 'A Harlequin Pembroke Table', with details of the mechanism for raising the till.*
Right, *Fig. 117: Inlaid satinwood Harlequin Pembroke table, a variation on the design in Fig. 116. Circa 1790; width open about 100 cm. (Phillips, Son & Neale.)*

actual draughtsmanship is little less important than the object portrayed, Sheraton concludes his address thus:

> . . . I only wish that a comparison be made with any other book hitherto published for the use of Cabinet-makers and Upholsterers, and then it will sufficiently speak for itself.

To this end, the bulk of the book is taken up with a lengthy illustrated treatise on geometry and perspective, and to stress his view of the importance of this aspect of his work it is prefaced by an allegorical frontispiece. It depicts some bearded toga-clad gentlemen demonstrating and drawing while

Cupid unfurls (or furls) a scroll, the whole being set in a room, open at one end and with a temple beyond, appropriately furnished in the 'Sheraton style'. Beneath are some lines of explanation:

> Time alters fashions and frequently obliterates the works of art and ingenuity; but that which is founded on Geometry & real Science, will remain unalterable.

The designs, like those in most earlier books, cover a wide range of articles. What proportion of them were the work of Sheraton himself, and which of them were derived from actual examples of the productions of other men is not easy to decide. He is quite open in giving credit where it is due, as, for instance, in the case of a library table-cum-steps of which he states: 'The design was taken from steps that have been made by Mr. Campbell, Upholsterer to the Prince of Wales. They were made for the King [George III] and highly approved by him, as every way answering the intended purpose.'

In a similar manner, Sheraton includes a double-page plate showing the four sides of a drawing-room. Of this, he remarks:

> To assist me in what I have shewn, I had the opportunity of seeing the Prince of Wales's, the Duke of York's, and other noblemen's drawing-rooms. I have not, however, followed any one in particular, but have furnished my ideas from the whole, with such particulars as I thought best suited to give a display of the present taste in fitting up such rooms. . . . A room of this description [that of the Prince] is not, however, a proper precedent for drawing-rooms in general, as it partakes principally of the character and ordinance of a state saloon-room, in which are entertained ambassadors, courtiers, and other personages of the highest stations.

The room in question, at Carlton House, measured no less than 48 ft. 6 in. by 34 ft., so it is understandable that an apology was made to less spaciously housed citizens.

Sheraton's designs are a further move

from the styles that had been popular in Chippendale's day, and a refinement of those shown by Hepplewhite only a few years earlier. Furnishings of the 1790's are plainer and lighter in pattern than those of the 1750's, and carving is mostly replaced by inlay and painting. Chairs that were

once of ample size become much smaller, and their backs more delicate (Fig. 113). Mahogany retained its devotees, but the most fashionable buyers preferred satinwood. It was brought to Britain from the Indies from about 1760, but was not employed in any quantity until a decade or so

Below, Fig. 118: Mahogany-framed Chamber-horse, the centre leg at the front pulling forward to steady the machine when it is in use. Circa 1790; width 75 cm. (John Keil, Ltd.)

Right, Fig. 119: Cabinet on stand, the legs of the latter headed by oval inlays of Prince of Wales' feathers. Circa 1790; width 50·8 cm. (John Keil, Ltd.)

later. Soon after that, another variety was imported from Ceylon. Both types tended to be brittle and show cracks unless carefully handled, and they were used principally as veneers. This was partly because more satisfactory results could be obtained from a carefully selected piece with good markings, but also because it was an expensive timber and veneering made a little go a long way. In his *Cabinet Dictionary* of 1803 Sheraton wrote enthusiastically of satin-wood, remarking that it had then been widely used for about 20 years and that it had 'a cool, light and pleasing effect in furniture'.

The direct influence of the *Drawing-Book* is to be seen today in a number of surviving articles conforming to designs in it. The 'Lady's Writing Table' in Fig. 115 is Plate 37 in the 1803 edition of Sheraton's volume, in which he wrote:

> The convenience of this table is, that a lady, when writing at it, may both receive the benefit of the fire, and have her face screened from the scorching heat.
>   The style of finishing them is neat, and rather elegant. They are frequently made of satin wood, cross-banded, japanned, and the top lined with green leather.

The present example is of mahogany with a slight inlay of light-coloured wood. The side boxes, which are shown in the open position, 'fly out by themselves, by the force of

Below, *Fig. 120: Tea caddy decorated with filigree paper and on the front a painting on silk. Circa 1790; width about 19 cm. (Private collection.)*

Right, *Fig. 121: Cabinet on a stand ornamented with filigree paper, coloured and gilt. Circa 1790; width 86·3 cm. (H. Blairman & Sons.)*

a common spring' when the knobs above them are pressed. In a like manner, the screen rises by means of concealed weights on pressing the disc in the centre at the back.

Such 'mechanical' pieces were much in demand at the time, but few of them have been preserved in full working order. Age and careless handling combine to weaken or

break springs, pivots and other moving parts, and once they cease to operate correctly they are usually cast aside as useless. The inspiration for such devices came from France and Germany, where they were equally popular, and the German writer, Sophie von la Roche, records a visit she made to one of her countrymen when she was in London in 1786. He was Merlin von Lüttich, known simply as 'Merlin', and he lived in Hanover Square, where she mentioned seeing, among other 'evidence of his labour and industry':

> Neat little writing- reading- or working-tables, combined with charming, soft-toned pianos . . . Others with the pianos concealed, and clever desks with lights attached for quartettes, set up in less than three minutes, which, if not required for music, might be converted into a nice piece of furniture for playing chess. A tea-table, where the housewife can open and close the cock of the tea-urn with her feet and rotate the table-disk to pour out the cups, and thus send tea and sugar round.[1]

Both Merlin and Sheraton catered for those who liked to take exercise within their own walls. Of the former, another caller at his establishment noticed:

> The portable hygæian chair, by which persons may swing themselves with safety, at Merlin's, are very clever, and the physicians say are extremely conducive to health; their motion I found easy and pleasing.[2]

The visit was made in 1788, and the writer recorded that the chairs cost £40 each: 'too expensive for most people merely for pleasure'.

Sheraton's contribution to the same end is a design for a 'Chamber Horse', the deep seat of which is filled with layers of springs affixed to boards. The moving portion is leather-covered, and the maker is warned:

> The leather at each end is cut in slits to give vent to the air, which would otherwise resist the motion downwards.

Another piece of furniture directly following a Sheraton design is the 'Cylinder Desk and Book case' in Fig. 114. The curved front is linked to the writing-surface within,

Below, *Fig. 124: An engraving from Ackermann's* Repository of Arts, *July 1811.* **Right**, *Plate 20: 'Metamorphic Library Chair . . . an elegant and truly comfortable armchair and a set of library steps', made by Morgan and Sanders. Circa 1810. (Private collection.)*

METAMORPHIC LIBRARY CHAIR.

[1] Op. cit., page 140.

[2] *Passages from the Diaries of Mrs. Philip Lybbe Powys*, ed. Emily J. Climenson, 1899, page 232.

so that when the cylinder is raised the flat surface slides forward. The engraved plate is dated 1792, and the author comments on the glass panes of the bookcase: 'The square figure of the door is much in fashion now.'

A by-way of furniture ornamentation was the use of paper filigree for the purpose. The craft originated probably in southern Europe, perhaps in the 16th Century, and was there employed for embellishing religious pictures and similar objects. English examples of the work dating from the late 17th Century have survived but are scarce,[1] and most extant specimens result from the revival that occurred between about 1780 and 1820.

The principal medium used took the form of long, narrow strips of paper, plain or

Below, *Fig. 125: Nest of cross-banded mahogany 'Quartetto Tables' of the type described and illustrated in Sheraton's* Cabinet Directory. *Circa 1800; width 54·5 cm.* (*John Keil, Ltd.*)

tinted or gilded on the edges, which were rolled or twisted as required. They were then glued to the surface to be decorated and the result was an unusual mosaic effect unlike anything else. Other materials were sometimes added: imitation pearls, fragments of mica and glass 'jewels', while small paintings on silk and coloured engravings were occasionally used to give further interest.

The work was sometimes executed by professionals, but was largely the province of ladies filling their leisure with what was a fashionable pursuit. They were led by Princess Elizabeth, the artistic third daughter of George III who is known to have obtained her supplies from the Royal cabinet-maker, Charles Elliott, of 97 New Bond Street. In 1791 she purchased from him a ready-made box and a tea-caddy together with supplies of filigree paper. Articles for decoration were made with sunken surfaces to receive the paper, and at least one of the magazines of the day printed instructions for its readers and provided patterns for them to copy.

The tea-caddy in Fig. 120 is a typical example of the work, and as it has been preserved with its original cardboard outer box the colours are almost as good as they were when it was made. More often, dust and dirt have wrought havoc and covered the fragile surfaces with an irremovable and unattractive brown stain.

On a larger scale than the foregoing is the cabinet in Fig. 121, of which the front centres on a circular representation of a basket of flowers. It is a considerable tour de force and must have occupied many months in the making. While the main groundwork comprises innumerable tiny rolls of paper, much ingenuity has been expended in forming swags, ovals and other shapes in an attempt to imitate or rival wood inlay.

[1] See Geoffrey Wills, *English Furniture, 1550–1760*, page 124.

11 : The Regency

STRICTLY speaking, the period known as The Regency should include only the years during which George, Prince of Wales, acted as Regent during the illness of his father, George III. This was from 1811 to 1820, when the Prince succeeded to the throne as George IV. In fact, the period has expanded to embrace a decade or so earlier and not infrequently an elastic number of years after the coronation. It is now a generic term, often with little precise reference to the Prince Regent himself or to his personal taste.

The Prince's true taste is epitomised in the Pavilion at Brighton, which is Oriental in its general appearance as well as its interior detail. William Hone published some satirical verses entitled 'The Joss and his Folly', which began:

Below, *Fig. 126: Caricature of George, Prince Regent, and the Brighton Pavilion, by George Cruikshank, 1820.*

> —The queerest of all the queer sights
>   I've set sight on;—
> Is the *what d'ye-call'-t thing*, here,
>   The Folly at Brighton
> The outside—huge teapots,
>   all drill'd round with holes,
> Relieved by extinguishers,
>   sticking on poles;
> The inside—all tea-things,
>   and dragons, and bells,
> The show rooms—*all* show,
>   the sleeping rooms—cells.
> But the *grand* Curiosity
>   's not to be seen—
> The owner himself—
>   an old fat Mandarin . . .

George Cruikshank's caricature which ac-

companied the lines is reproduced in Fig. 126.[1]

The Regency style, however, derived from no farther East than Greece, and its Chinese variation was little more than a personal whim of the Prince and his imitators. The mid-18th-Century classical revival was owed to the activities of Robert Adam, but this fresh fashion was pursued with greater seriousness. Its initiation and early development in England were due to the architect, Henry Holland, who was responsible for the refurbishing of Carlton House when it came into the possession of the Prince of Wales in 1783.

French taste had been continually influencing the design of English furniture throughout the 18th Century, and this took place despite the fact that the countries were actively at war with one another for much of the time. In the 1770's not only were French chairs, commodes, tapestries

---

[1] *The Queen's Matrimonial Ladder*, 1820.

Left, *Plate 21: Rosewood dwarf cupboard, the frieze inlaid with brass and the doors flanked by Egyptian terms. Circa 1815; width 94 cm. (Private collection.)*

Below, *Fig. 127: Tambour-fronted cylinder bureau of rosewood inlaid with ivory, and the drawers fitted with ivory knob handles, in the style of Henry Holland. Circa 1800; width 124·5 cm. (H. Blairman & Sons.)*

and other articles brought across the Channel, but close copies of them were being made in London. With the storming of the Bastille in 1789 and the ensuing Revolution, the pro- and anti-French factions, which had for long been active in England, grew farther apart.

The Tories of the day were ever anxious that Gallic licence should not affect the inhabitants of their own country, while the Whigs made no effort to hide their admiration for the aspirations of the revolutionaries. Filial duty did not come easily to the the Prince of Wales and, opposed to his

father in most things he allied himself with the Whig party. As circumstances had led Henry Holland to working for many of them, it was without doubt for this reason he was selected to carry out the work at Carlton House.

Holland began his career as a landscape gardener, working as the partner and assistant of Lancelot 'Capability' Brown; the man who earned his sobriquet because he invariably saw the 'capability' of a project. Holland did not visit France until after the start of the Revolution, but there was no shortage of French models for him to study

Below, *Fig. 128: Interior of a room in the Egyptian style at Deepdene, Surrey, from Thomas Hope's* Household Furniture, 1807. *(Photograph: H. Blairman & Sons.)*

Right, *Fig. 129: Breakfront bookcase inlaid with Grecian motifs and applied with Egyptian heads, the whole standing on lions' paw feet. Circa 1805; width about 220 cm. (Mallett & Son, Ltd.)*

without stirring from London. While he was responsible for supervising the work at Carlton House, the interior decorations were largely in the hands of a Frenchman who was described in documents as 'William Gaubert, of Panton Street, Maker of Ornamental Furniture'.[1]

Horace Walpole paid a visit to the mansion in September 1785, and recorded a description of what he saw there in a letter to the Countess of Upper Ossory. 'We went', he wrote

> to see the Prince's new palace in Pall Mall; and were charmed. It will be the most perfect in Europe. There is an august simplicity that astonished me.

You cannot call it magnificent; it is the taste and propriety that strike. Every ornament is at a proper distance, and not too large, but all delicate and new, with more freedom and variety than Greek ornaments; and, though probably borrowed from the Hôtel de Condé and other new palaces, not one that is not rather classic than French.[2]

The craftsmen and traders supplying the young Prince had from the start included a

---

[1] H. Clifford Smith, op. cit., page 101.

[2] *Letters*, op. cit., Vol. XIII, page 320.

Below, *Fig. 130: Couch or day bed designed by Henry Hope for his house at Deepdene, Surrey, see Fig. 128. Circa 1805; width 162·5 cm. (H. Blairman & Sons.)*

Right, *Fig. 131: Rosewood occasional table inlaid with brass Grecian patterns, the shelf supports in the form of kneeling Egyptians and the base applied with Oriental dragons. Circa 1810; width about 70 cm. (Mallett & Son, Ltd.)*

Above, *Fig. 132: Painted armchair with cane back and seat, the frame stamped J G, for John Gee, Turner and Chair maker to George III. Circa 1810. (Bearnes & Waycotts.)* **Right,** *Fig. 133: Chair of classical pattern in the manner of Thomas Hope. Circa 1805. (H. Blairman & Sons.)*

mission from the Prince of Wales had been for 'Carving and gilding done by S. Nelson, by order of Mr. Degare', for which he was paid £1,659, and by 1795 he was owed no less than £15,500 'for furniture sold to H:R:H: and delivered to Carleton House'.[2]

A government Commission endeavoured to clear up the Prince's tangled finances, and had Daguerre's account examined by Ince and Mayhew as regards the furniture and by Matthew Boulton for the metal wares. Some idea of the scale of the purchases can be gained from the fact that Henry Holland was owed £3,854, a sum that included several years' arrears of his £100 per annum salary as Superintendent of the Works, a claim by the Royal hosier amounted to £1,601, and Mrs. Urania Devins was owed £1,050 for the supply of perfumes. Daguerre's total of £15,500 must have represented a great quantity of furnishings.

In the final years of the 18th Century French taste began to show a change, the principal exponents of the newer style being two architects, Pierre-François-Léonard Fountaine and Charles Percier. In 1801 they published a large volume of designs for all kinds of articles from vases to screens, which show an increased interest in classical forms and ornament:[3] designs that

sprinkling of expatriate Frenchmen, and by 1789 he was employing the eminent Parisian *marchand-mercier*, Dominique Daguerre; in the rue Saint-Honoré, under the sign *A la Couronne d'Or*, his clients ranged from the French royalty and nobility to the wealthiest inhabitants of Russia and England. In 1788 he had succeeded to an already established business, but five years later he fled to London, where he was joined by Martin-Eloy Lignereux, who was a cabinet-maker.

The *marchand-merciers* (literally translatable as 'merchants'-merchants') dealt not only in fine furniture but supplied porcelain, bronzes and other types of luxuries, and have been described as being equivalent to a modern combination of antique-dealer and interior-decorator.[1] Daguerre's first com-

[1] F. J. B. Watson, *Louis XVI Furniture*, 1960, page 78.

[2] H. Clifford Smith, op. cit., page 109.

[3] Published in Paris, the full title of the work is: *Receuil de décorations, intérieures, comprenant tout ce qui rapport à l'ameublement, comme vases, trépieds, candelabres, cassolettes, lustres, tables, secrétaires, lits, canapés, fauteuils, chaises, tabourets, miroirs, écrans, etc.*

flourished during the heyday of the Emperor Napoleon and received the name of 'Empire'.

Aɴᴀʟᴏɢᴏᴜѕ to the activities of Fountaine and Percier a movement was occurring in England under the leadership of Henry Holland, in whose office was a young man names Charles Heathcote Tatham. Holland befriended him, and sent him to the Mediterranean to study as part of his training. The two corresponded for much of the three years Tatham spent in Italy, and the student sent back drawings of what he saw and considered adaptable to the taste of the time. In 1796 he wrote to say how interested he was to learn of the prevailing enthusiasm for the Greek style, which he heard 'is gaining ground in England'. It encouraged him to publish in 1799 illustrations of what he considered to be worthy examples of classical work.[1]

In 1796 Henry Holland was entrusted with the task of redecorating Southill, Bedfordshire, the home of the Whig brewer, Samuel

Below, *Fig. 134: Mahogany 'library table' supplied to Sir Richard Colt Hoare by Thomas Chippendale the Younger in 1805. Width 244 cm. (Stourhead, Wiltshire: The National Trust.)*

[1] *Etchings of Ancient Ornamental Architecture drawn from the Originals in Rome and Other Parts of Italy*, second edition 1803, third edition 1810.

Whitbread. Here he made considerable use of dark-coloured wood in contrast with delicate gilt mounts, and although Greek details, such as a use of the anthemion motif, are present, the general form is frequently of French origin. Sometimes (Fig. 127), only the employment of rosewood in England differentiates the pieces being made on each side of the Channel. The dark brown timber with black markings began to supplant satinwood increasingly as the turn of the century approached, when its importation from Brazil and the Indies grew in volume. While it had been used occasionally in the 1750's, its presence is almost a trade-mark of better quality Regency furniture.

Much of the furniture designed by Henry Holland was made by Marsh and Tatham of Mount Street, of whom the latter was the brother of Tatham the architect. Marsh was established as early as 1778, and with various changes of partners the firm carried on for several decades. Examples of their work are still at Southill, while some of their furniture supplied to Carlton House and Brighton Pavilion, under the names of Tatham & Bailey and Bailey & Saunders, is now at Buckingham Palace.

In 1806 Holland died, aged 61, but the

Below, Fig. 135: Mahogany kidney-shaped table on flat end supports linked by a turned stretcher. Circa 1810; width 167·6 cm. (Private collection.)

Regency style was established and continued to flourish for at least two further decades. A year later another furniture-designer rose to the forefront. He was Henry Hope, a rich dilettante of Anglo-Scottish origin, who had come to England and proceeded to embellish his London home in Duchess Street, and his country home at Deepdene, Surrey, in a manner that inspired considerable comment. One visitor to Duchess Street in 1804 remarked that 'it certainly excited no feelings of comfort as a dwelling', while Hope himself was dubbed by Sydney Smith 'The man of chairs and tables, the gentleman of sofas'.

Thomas Hope published a number of illustrated works which showed the interiors of his houses, as well as others depicting classical scenes. The best-known of them is his *Household Furniture and Interior Decoration*, of 1807. The chair in Fig. 133 follows a Hope design and is a copy of a type favoured in ancient Greece and Rome, with a curved back decorated in the manner of vase-painting. Although archaeologically almost impeccable it promises little comfort, and its purpose was mainly to occupy a place in the formal decorative scheme.

Fashionable interest, while it concentrated on classical forms did not hesitate to ally them with others. This occurred in particular with Egyptian ornament, which had become popular following Napoleon's campaign in Egypt. Bonaparte's entourage included Baron Denon who published a two-volume book on his travels, which had an influence throughout Europe. One result was a room designed by Hope and illustrated in his *Household Furniture* (Fig. 128), from which a couch is shown in Fig. 130. In both the couch, or day-bed, and the bookcase in Fig. 129 an amalgam of Greek and Egyptian is to be seen, while in the small table in Fig. 131 is a third element mixed with the others: Chinese.

A MONG the 18th-Century cabinet-makers whose businesses were carried on into the Regency, that of Thomas Chippendale is to be numbered. When he died in 1779 his eldest son, also named Thomas, was thirty years of age, and with his father's partner Thomas Haig he continued the workshops and showroom in St. Martin's Lane. Of the firm's later clients probably Sir Richard Colt Hoare is the best known, as his purchases remain *in situ* at Stourhead, Wiltshire, where visitors to what is

Below, *Fig. 136: Mahogany dumb-waiter with brass pierced galleries and turned uprights, the tripod base with reeded legs and brass cap castors.* Circa *1815; diameter 55·2 cm. (Private collection.)* **Right**, *Fig. 137: Parcel-gilt mahogany armchair supplied by Thomas Chippendale the Younger in 1812. Height 95 cm. (Stourhead, Wiltshire: The National Trust.)*

now a property of the National Trust can see them.

The chair and gout stool illustrated in Plate 16 were supplied to Stourhead by Thomas Chippendale the Younger in 1802, with the former invoiced as follows:

> 6 sattin wood elbow chairs with black ebony bands, caned seats, turned legs and on casters   £31.10.0.

In the Library of the same house is the desk in Fig. 134, which is ornamented indiscriminately with classical heads at each side and

Below, *Fig. 138: Davenport of rosewood inlaid with brass lines.* Circa *1810; width 45·7 cm. (Mallett & Son, Ltd.)*

Right, *Plate 22: Carved rosewood chair, the seat covered in gros point needlework.* Circa *1830; height 88 cm. (Private collection.)*

Egyptian ones at each end. It was described in a bill of 1805 as:

> A large mahogany library table with pedestals and drawers under pedestals, mahogany panelled doors, thermed legs with philosopher's heads carved on d°., four end therms with Egyptian heads   £115.0.0.

At Stourhead also is the armchair in Fig. 137, as well as a number of other pieces. All exhibit a high standard of craftmanship worthy of the famous name of their supplier.

The retirement of Thomas Haig took place in 1796, and in the same year he made a will bequeathing to his former partner the sum of £1,000. Later, in 1802, a codicil made it plain that Chippendale was indebted to Haig, and the latter's executors were directed not to pay the £1,000 unless all the monies owing to Haig were paid within a period of a twelvemonth. In 1804 Chippendale was declared bankrupt and the stock at St. Martin's Lane was sold by auction; the second time this had occurred within a period of under 40 years (see page 13). The dispersal of made-up goods and raw timber occupied a total of five days, and the former included:

> . . . many articles of great taste and the finest workmanship: commodes, chiffoniers, chests of drawers; sofa, card, writing and several sets of dining and breakfast tables, of large and small dimensions on pillars and claws; gentlemen's and ladies' dressing d°.; cheval glasses, sideboards and pedestals.

Amongst the timber was:

> . . . very valuable Jamaica, Spanish, Cuba and Honduras mahogany in planks and boards; choice Satin, Rose and Kingswood, Cedar in logs, Walnut-tree, American Birch; and a selection of the most beautiful veneers of extraordinary dimensions and very scarce.

An artist who was said by one of his contemporaries to possess great ability as a

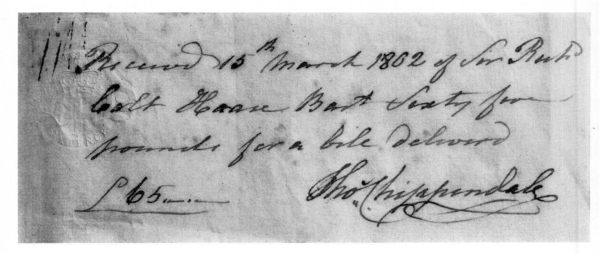

draughtsman and designer, Chippendale exhibited at the Royal Academy between 1784 and 1801. A modern writer voiced the opinion that he had 'an advantage over most of his fellow-exhibitors in that he could, if necessary, have his frames made at home.[1]

He apparently recovered from the blow of bankruptcy and recommenced business. In 1817 he had premises in the Haymarket, and in an 1821 directory is entered as an upholsterer at 42 Jermyn Street. In 1822 he died, aged 73.

As was the case in earlier periods it is only rarely possible to name the makers of Regency furniture, and most of it remains anonymous. Not all pieces made at the time were as obviously in the Regency style as others, and there can be little doubt that many buyers were content with articles of plain appearance. Sheraton showed designs for kidney-shaped tables, and the example in Fig. 135 owes much more to a pencil than it does to that of Holland or Hope. Likewise, the two-tier dumb-waiter in Fig. 136, is functional and unpretentious.

The foregoing pieces were made of mahogany, but rosewood was employed in making equally modest-looking articles; many of them attractive to modern eyes because of their simple lines and convenient size. The Davenport in Fig. 138, is a good example. These neat desks were apparently named after a Captain Davenport, who ordered the very first one from Gillows in the late 18th Century and his name has been inseparable from them ever since.

[1] William T. Whitley, *Artists and their Friends in England, 1700–1799*, 2 vols., 1928, Vol. II, page 262.

12 : The Regency II

CABINET-MAKERS of both British and French origin were active in London in the early years of the 19th Century. The latter had left their native land during the troubled times of the Revolution and set up workshops in London, where, as had been done by their predecessors a century or so before, they introduced new ideas.

Among them was Louis-Constantin Le Gaigneur, who established himself at 19 Queen Street, Edgware Road, in premises which he named the Buhl Manufactory. Predictably, he specialised in metal inlay of the type for which André-Charles Boulle had been famous in the late 17th/early 18th Century. Work of the kind continued to appeal to French buyers even after the long-lived Boulle had died at the age of 90 in 1732, and a number of makers worked in the style throughout the century. Le Gaigneur followed in the tradition.

A kneehole writing-table in the Wallace Collection, London, was at one time accepted as being of the Louis XIV period, but in the present century it was examined closely and found to bear a pewter plaque inscribed: 'Louis Le Gaigneur fecit'. Two similar pieces, also signed, are at Windsor Castle, and it is known that the Prince Regent made purchases from Le Gaigneur in about 1815. His work differs in an essential particular from that executed in Paris: the English-made articles are veneered on a carcass of pine, whereas in France the wood used would have been oak.[1]

Brass inlay in the Boulle manner became very popular as part of the ornament on English pieces from the first years of the 19th Century, and was especially effective against the contrasting dark background of rosewood. The dwarf cabinet illustrated on page 162 has a frieze of foliate scroll pattern as well as a conventional floral design on the fronts of the flanking uprights. Both patterns are completely unrelated to the Egyptian heads and feet that surmount and

---

[1] F. J. B. Watson, op. cit., 1956, page 244.

terminate the end members; a juxtaposition not at all uncommon during the period.

The cutting and application of metal inlay would undoubtedly have been a special branch of the cabinet-making industry, and all except the biggest workshops would have sub-contracted it to men who did nothing else. According to one writer 'the presence of this brass inlay on furniture is evidence of origin in London; for such metal work was a specialised trade, carried on in London in the neighbourhood of St. Martin's Lane and Long Acre'.[1] No reason was given for making the suggestion, but as the district was the cabinet-making centre it may have been no more than guesswork. A classified directory for 1821, doubtless compiled in the preceding year, lists two men under the heading 'Buhl Manufactuers'.[2] They are:

Binns Joseph, 5 Frederick pl, Goswell st road
Parker Thomas, 22 Warwick st, Golden square

It is uncertain whether they made complete articles or inlaid panels to the order of other men. Neither of them, it may be noticed, was in the area of St. Martin's Lane and Long Acre.

A stimulus to the employment of Egyptian devices was provided by the exploits of Admiral Nelson. His outstanding victory at the Battle of the Nile on 1st August 1798 was eventually followed by his absolute defeat of the French at Trafalgar in 1805. His sudden death in action at the very moment of triumph, secured his position as a national hero. The occasional appearance of a crocodile, rather an unlikely choice as a decorative adjunct, is said to be a symbol of the Nile, where the British sailors would have seen them basking on the banks of the river. Similarly, the rope-like turning or carving often found in chair-backs (Fig. 142) is said to have been inspired by the Navy and the enormous national interest shown then in maritime affairs.

Left, *Plate 23: Two piano stools—(Back) mahogany with four turned and curved supports. Circa 1810; diameter 35 cm. (Front) walnut with carved stem and tripod base. Circa 1850; diameter 35 cm. (Private collection.)* **Above,** *Fig. 140: Cross-banded rosewood sofa- and games-table. Circa 1800; width open 155 cm. (Phillips, Son & Neale.)*

More definitely with a Nelsonian association is a suite which was presented to Greenwich Hospital in 1815 in memory of the Admiral, and is now in the Admiralty.

[1] Margaret Jourdain, *Regency Furniture*, revised edition 1949, page 15.

[2] *Robson's Classification of Trades and London Commercial Directory.* The term 'Buhl' was often used in the 19th Century as an alternative to 'Boulle'.

It is carved with dolphins, the ubiquitous acanthus, and ribbed cornucopias, while the settee has tall, curled ends that make it look a somewhat uninviting piece of seat furniture with little promise of comfort.[1]

More restrained in design than the foregoing is the 'Grecian Couch' in Fig. 141. It is made of beechwood, japanned black with the moulded edges gilt and with gilt metal mounts. Similar couches, or day beds,

must have existed in their hundreds, and were to be found in homes on both sides of the English Channel. The now well-known picture of Madame Récamier, painted by Jacques-Louis David and now in the Louvre, shows the beautiful wife of the

---

[1] The suite is illustrated in Clifford Musgrave, *Regency Furniture*, 1961, Plate 11.

Below, *Fig. 141: 'Grecian' couch of japanned beechwood, partly gilt with gilt metal mounts. Circa 1810; length about 200 cm. (Private collection.)*

Right, *Fig. 142: Mahogany chair with moulded 'sabre' legs and rope-carved bar in the back, the top rail inset with brass lines. Circa 1810. (Private collection.)*

banker reclining on a comparable piece of furniture.

While large-sized bookcases continued to be made (see page 165) there was a big demand for sets of open shelves standing about 3 feet in height and a foot or so wider. Revolving tiered book-holders were also made, but are now scarce and were perhaps never plentiful on account of the expense of their comparatively complex construction. The example in Fig. 145 is a copy of one illustrated in an engraving published in Ackermann's *Repository of the Arts* in 1810. An accompanying note points out that the design is owed to the earlier dumb-waiter (page 136), and adds:

> This bookcase appears to afford some valuable conveniences, as, for instance, it may be placed in a recess, or corner of a room in which from local circumstances it might be inconvenient or impossible to dispose the same number of books.

The most typical article of Regency furniture is perhaps the sofa table. It evolved from the Pembroke table, and Sheraton stated that it was used 'before a sofa and generally made between five and six feet long and from twenty-two inches to two feet broad'. An inlaid rosewood example is illustrated in Fig. 140, the central portion of the top being removable and reversible to reveal a chess or draughts board and a surface lined with leather marked for backgammon.

A variant of the sofa table is the games-cum-writing table in Fig. 143. It is one of a few of the same design which have been recorded, and is unique among them because it bears the label of its maker. The small oblong of printed paper is gummed to the side of a well disclosed when the top is slid out, and it is remarkable that the label was overlooked until recently in spite of the fact that the table has been illustrated in books and periodicals since the 1920's. The label bears the wording:

Manufactured and Sold by J. M'Lane & Son, Pancrass Street, Tottenham Court-Road, and 58, Upper Mary-le-bone-street, Portland-Place.

In 1803 Thomas Sheraton gave the addresses of the firm as Upper Terrace, Tottenham Court Road and 34 Marylebone Street, Piccadilly. Other sources name them variously as 'J^{no}. M'Clean' and 'John McLean & Son', and in the first instance with premises in Little Newport Street, Leicester Square. It appears likely that John M'Clean of Little Newport Street, who was there as early as 1774, had no direct connection with the others, or with William M'Lean who was at 58 Marylebone

Street in 1825. The latter was probably the 'Son' on the label on the table. A further labelled piece from the same source is the circular-topped writing-table in Fig. 144, which dates from about 1810.

IN the Regency period the frames of looking-glasses followed other furnishings and became completely changed in style. The ovals which had been so popular with Robert Adam and his followers were banished, and simple rectangles replaced them. Three-panel overmantel glasses and smaller ones with a single plate of glass both followed a uniform pattern. In the majority

Below, *Fig. 144: Circular-topped table on a tripod base, of mahogany with mounts of gilt metal, by J. M'Lane & Son. Circa 1810; diameter 106·7 cm. (Saltram, Devon: The National Trust.)*

of instances the giltwood frame had upright reeded, moulded or plain columns with Corinthian capitals, while along the top ran a frieze. This was varied in depth, with shallow ones displaying Wedgwood-like classical figures in relief and deeper examples varying in treatment but often framing a transfer-painting or a panel of *verre églomisé*.[1] Egyptian motifs were

---

[1] Transfer paintings were made by sticking a print behind glass, rubbing off the paper and roughly painting the remaining engraved lines. *Verre églomisé* was made by gilding on the back of a sheet of glass, making a pattern by engraving the gold leaf and filling-in the background with colour or, frequently, black.

Below, *Fig. 145: Mahogany tiered revolving bookcase, after a design published in 1810. Height about 200 cm. (Phillips, Son & Neale.)*

Right, *Fig. 146: Set of open bookshelves, painted to simulate rosewood.* Circa 1810; width about 70 cm. (Mallett & Son, Ltd.)

sometimes employed, and no doubt once helped the article to form part of a complete decorative scheme.

Probably, the most typical mirrors of the period are the convexes: circular and outward curving, and which, in Sheraton's words, 'strengthen the colour and take off the coarseness of objects by contracting them'. They were very fashionable in 1803, when the *Cabinet Dictionary* was published, and it was found that 'the perspective of rooms in which they are suspended presents itself on the surface and produces an agreeable effect'.

Such glasses were not new to the Regency, but had been included as early as 1762 in Ince and Mayhew's *Universal System*. One of the plates in the book is entitled 'Frames for Convex or Concave Glasses', and depicts eight designs composed of 'C'-curves, twisted rope, or entwined ribbons, and one formed of an arrangement of flowers and rope dangling from the beak of a bird with outspread wings hanging uncomfortably upside down. The authors commented that they 'have a very pretty Effect in a well furnish'd Room'. While the publication of design books cannot be accepted as positive evidence that articles were actually made, there are a number of extant convexes datable to before 1800. Some that actually existed in a house and have since disappeared are listed in an inventory made in about 1780 of the contents of Appuldurcombe Park, Isle of Wight, the seat of Sir Richard Worsley. In the Drawing room were:

> 2 round convex Mirrors in carv'd & gilt frames, plates 2 ft. diameter.[1]

The house was furnished by Thomas

---

[1] L. O. J. Boynton, 'Sir Richard Worsley's Furniture at Appuldurcombe Park', in *Furniture History*, I (1965), page 44.

Above, *Fig. 147: Convex mirror in a giltwood frame with ebonised inner slip, with the label of Thomas Fentham, 136 Strand, London.* Circa *1810. (Phillips, Son & Neale.)*

Right, *Fig. 148: Cabinet, parcel-gilt and decorated with 'inlaying' of Chinese design.* Circa *1820; width about 110 cm. (Mallett & Son, Ltd.)*

Chippendale, and doubtless he provided the two convexes.

Although rosewood was most fashionable, not everyone was able to afford its cost and resort was therefore had to imitation. This was achieved with some success by the skilful use of stains and varnish, as in a receipt printed in 1825:

To imitate Rose-wood.
Take half a pound of log-wood, boil it with three pints of water till it is of a very dark red, to which add about half an ounce of salt of tartar, and when boiling hot stain your wood with two or three coats, taking care that it is nearly

dry between each; then with a stiff flat brush, such as you use for graining, make streaks with a very deep black stain, which, if carefully executed, will be very near the appearance of dark rose-wood.[1]

Much of the simulated rosewood furniture was made of beech, a wood normally liable to attack by worm. However, the coating that deceives the human eye appears also to deter the wood-worm, which often avoids such pieces. When in good condition, unchipped, and smoothly polished through generations of handling and dusting, furniture of this kind can prove remarkably like the real article. Sometimes the deception is revealed only by the noticeably light weight of most woods in comparison with rosewood. Use of the latter for making chairs has often proved self-destructive, for the very weight of a rosewood one can result in the top-rail becoming detached when the chair is lifted.

Another type of painted decoration was done in imitation of inlaid ebony and ivory, sometimes termed 'Pen-painting' and in a book of 1835, 'Inlaying'. The work was executed on a thin ground of white gesso, or occasionally direct on white wood, by carefully drawing in a black ink and then finishing with one or more coats of clear varnish. Over the years the latter has nearly always turned to a pale yellow-brown tint, but where there has not been direct exposure to light and dirt the original contrasting black and white are to be seen. Tables, cabinets and other pieces of furniture were decorated in this manner, and smaller objects such as work-boxes were also produced. The latter were perhaps the product of amateurs, for whose benefit a small book on this and allied types of decoration was published in 1835, the author being a Mr. B. F. Gandee who added

---

[1] Anon., *The Painter's and Varnisher's Pocket Manual*, 1825, page 160.

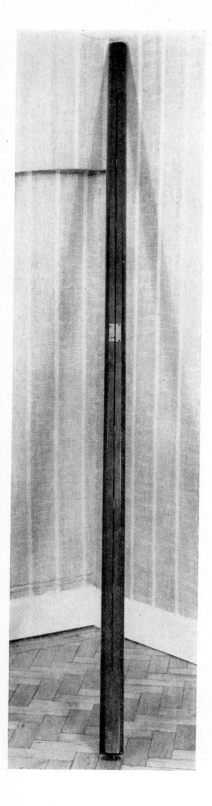

after his name the description 'Teacher'.[1] At the back of the volume he offered to give further instruction in any of the crafts he had described, and could supply original drawings from which to copy as well as 'a complete set of materials for Inlaying' at a cost of 10/6d.

Gandee included two engravings of designs for the work, both of them derived from the Chinese with figures surrounded by deep floral borders. Extant examples are in some cases of oriental pattern (Fig. 148), but others owe nothing to the East except for original conception of engraved ivory.

Another type of painted decoration is both rarer and more colourful than the foregoing. Again, it occurs on different varieties of furniture, and has been recorded on large pieces such as bureau-bookcases and cabinets. The work is carried out in minute detail and is obviously inspired by Persian painting of the type often seen on papier-mâché. It is likely that its production was owed to the presence in London of the Persian Ambassador, Abul-Hassan Quan, who arrived in the city and on 17 January 1810 was received by Queen Charlotte, 'with the same pomp and form as if her Majesty was holding a public drawing-room'. A fortnight later he was introduced to the Prince of Wales at Carlton House, and was presented with 'a very beautiful and curious clock, invented by Mr. Congreve, in which the time is measured by the

---

[1] B. F. Gandee, *The Artist, or Young Lady's Instructor*, 1835. The title-page and frontispiece of the book are early examples of George Baxter's method of colour-printing.

rotation of a platina ball'.[1] Interest in the country was further kindled by the publications of J. J. Morier, who had been there as a member of a mission.

For those who ventured abroad there were firms who made portable furniture that was easy to transport on both sea and land. Of them, Messrs. Morgan and Sanders, of Catherine Street, Strand, are remembered for their explicit trade-card or handbill page 192. Their principal clients would have been among the hundreds who voyaged annually to India, and took with them as much as possible that would be useful in their new life. The advertisement stated:

> These elegant Four Post and Tent Bedsteads, with Lath or Sacking bottom, made upon the best & most approved principle, are fixed up or taken down, in a few minutes, without the use of Tools . . . [The] very convenient & highly approved of Sofa Bed, contrived on purpose for Captains Cabins, & Ladies or Gentlemen, going to the East or West Indies; with every other Article necessary for Voyages & use of Foreign Climates: Mosquito Nett Furniture, Bedding, &c.—— The above Inventions & Improvements, with every other Article, in the Upholstery & Cabinet Branches, executed in the first stile of elegance & fashion.

Morgan and Sanders catered for officers engaged in the Peninsular War, who cam-

---

[1] The Ambassador ordered a large service from the Derby Manufactory of which there is a plate in the British Museum. His portrait was painted on Barr, Flight and Barr, Worcester porcelain, as were portraits of the Shah, Futteh Ali, and his son, Abbas Mirza. Congreve devised his 'rolling ball' clock in 1808, and the example of it presented by him to the Prince of Wales is in the Rotunda at Woolwich.

paigned accompanied by what would now be considered hopelessly bulky, heavy and superfluous equipment. The two-part chest of drawers, usually known as a 'military chest', was taken from camp to camp filled with the owner's clothing and other possessions. Some of the chests comprised plain drawers, but others included a secretaire with a leather-lined falling front (Fig. 151).

All are distinguished by a lack of any ornamentation except for the brass inset folding handles and, in most instances, brass protectors at the corners and short removable turned feet. They were made throughout the 19th Century, and as their design scarcely changed from one decade to another it is not always easy to date them closely.

Below, *Fig. 151: Mahogany campaign chest in two parts with one drawer fitted as a secretaire. Circa 1802; width 102 cm. (Private collection.)*

Right, *Plate 24: Rosewood games-table, the top inset with coloured squares of marble. Circa 1821 (see Fig. 152); width 74 cm. (Private collection.)*

MORGAN and SANDERS'S

Manufactory for their New Invented Imperial Dining Tables

AND PORTABLE CHAIRS,

The best & most approved SOFA BEDS, CHAIR BEDS, PATENT BRASS SCREW

FOUR POST & TENT BEDSTEADS, with Furniture and Bedding complete, at their

UPHOLSTERY and CABINET WARE-ROOMS

Catherine **16 & 17** *Street,*

Three doors from the Strand.

LONDON.

PATENT CAMP BEDS.   ARMY & NAVY EQUIPAGE.

Morgan and Sanders's, New Invented,

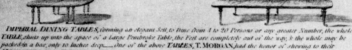

IMPERIAL DINING TABLES, *forming an elegant Sett, to Dine from 4 to 20 Persons or any greater Number, the whole TABLE shuts up into the space of a Large Pembroke Table, the Feet are completely out of the way, & the whole may be packed in a box, only 10 Inches deep. One of the above TABLES, T. MORGAN had the honor of shewing to their MAJESTIES & the PRINCESSES, at Buckingham House who according to their accustomed goodness, of encouraging Ingenuity, were most graciously pleased to express their highest approbation & sanction of the same.*

PORTABLE CHAIRS, *plain & with Arms, of Mahogany, or elegantly Japand, made to any pattern, a dozen of which pack in the space of two common Chairs.*

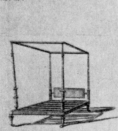

The best & most approved SOFA BEDS, forming an elegant SOFA, & may be transformed with great ease into a complete FOUR POST BED, with Bedding Furniture &c.

The best & most approved CHAIR BEDS, forming a handsome easy CHAIR, & is with great ease transformed into a TENT BED, with Furniture & Bedding complete.

PATENT BRASS SCREW BEDSTEADS, IN EVERY RESPECT SUPERIOR TO ALL OTHERS.

These elegant FOUR POST & TENT BEDSTEADS, with Lath or Sacking bottom, made upon the best & most approved principle, are fixed up or taken down, in a few minutes, without the use of Tools. The Furnitures are made upon a New Plan, of taking off or on, without Tools, Tacks, &c.

A very convenient & highly approved of SOFA BED, contrived on purpose for Captains Cabins, & Ladies or Gentlemen, going to the East or West Indies; with every other Article necessary for Voyages & use of Foreign Climates Musquito Net Furniture, Bedding, &c. The above Inventions & Improvements, with every other Article, in the UPHOLSTERY & CABINET BRANCHES, executed in the first stile of elegance & fashion.

13 : George Smith & J. C. Loudon

T HE firm of Morgan and Sanders, whose trade-card is shown on page 192 did not confine itself to supplying portable furniture. It also made a number of ingeniously contrived articles, which included what was called 'Pitt's Cabinett Globe Writing Table' (Figs. 155 and 156). The table was devised by a man named George Remington

Left, Fig. 152: Trade-card or hand-bill of Morgan and Sanders, Catherine Street, London, showing their portable furniture. Circa 1815. (Photograph: The Connoisseur.*) Below, Fig. 153: Note pasted inside the drawer of the table in Plate 24.*

who was granted a patent for it, and examples made by Morgan and Sanders were illustrated and described in Ackermann's *Repository of Arts* in 1810. At the time, one was bought by Queen Charlotte as a gift for one of her daughters, and is still at Buckingham Palace. When opened it becomes a sewing table, while another specimen in the Metropolitan Museum of Art, New York, combines facilities for both sewing and writing.

Shortly before the date of the Queen's purchase, George Smith, a cabinet-maker with premises in Prince's Street, Cavendish Square, issued the first of his books of designs. It was entitled *A Collection of Designs for Household Furniture and Interior Decoration*, of which the author wrote that they were 'studied from the best antique examples of the Egyptian, Greek and Roman styles' while he included for full measure a few of Chinese inspiration.[1]

---

[1] See *Regency Furniture Designs 1803–1862*, edited with an introduction by John Harris, 1961, in which are reprinted all the plates from Smith's 1808 *Designs* as well as a selection from Hope, and others.

Smith was indebted to Thomas Hope for many of his ideas, and both men favoured the use of human- and animal-headed legs with which to support tables and chairs. In the case of animals, the favourites were lions, whose realistic masks were carved at the tops of cranked leg-like members ending in equally realistic paws. His designs, on the whole, are fussy, especially when compared with many of those current less than a decade before and they portend the profusion of ornament that became common as the years advanced.

In 1826, Smith, whose address was then 41 Brewer Street, Golden Square, published a further volume, *The Cabinet-makers' and Upholsterers' Guide, Drawing Book and Repository of New and Original Designs for Household Furniture*. He recorded in it that the designs in his 1808 volume had become out of date, and he showed revised versions of them, as well as some with Gothic and Rococo features. Although he described himself as 'furniture draughtsman to his Majesty', proudly stated that he had supplied goods to the Royal family and had received the approbation of Thomas Hope, none of his furniture has been positively identified.

By the mid-1820's George IV had been crowned, his acrimonious battle with his wife had been resolved by her demise, and the King spent much of his time travelling between Brighton and Windsor in company with Lady Conyngham. His influence on the design of furniture, which had been so strong thirty years before, when he was Prince of Wales, had waned. Patronage for artists and cabinet-makers was now being drawn principally from the nobility and others.

Current designs are to be seen in three books which appeared within a few years of each other. They were:

The Rudiments of Drawing Cabinet and Upholstery Furniture, by Richard Brown, 1820, with a second edition two years later.

Left, *Plate 25: Mahogany tray-top table. Circa 1835; top 88·7 × 60·5 cm. (Private collection.)*

Above, *Fig. 154: 'A Music Chair', designed by Henry Whitaker.*

The Practical Cabinet Maker, Upholsterer and Complete Decorator, by a father and son, Peter and Michael Angelo Nicholson, 1826.
Designs of Cabinet and Upholstery Furniture in the Most Modern Style, by Henry Whitaker, 1825.

All three show the popularity of mouldings composed of deeply-cut reeding.[1] As al-

---

[1] The peculiarities of style of these and other designers of the period are summarised in Brian Reade, *Regency Antiques*, 1953.

ways, there was something to suit all tastes, from simple pieces which were sometimes poorly finished, to others laden with carving and exhibiting all the craftsman's skill.

The latter were plentiful, and those who were in business in London in 1817 have been culled from the pages of the Post Office directory for that year and reprinted.[1]

Below, *Fig. 155: A variation of 'Pitt's Cabinett Globe Writing Table', fitted as a sewing-table. The supports have giltwood Egyptian heads and lions' paw feet. Circa 1810; height 94 cm. (John Keil, Ltd.)*

That earlier fashions were not completely swept aside in later years is clear from the chance finding of the name of an inlaying specialist who is recorded in the 1825 issue of the same directory:

> Wilkinson P, Ornamental Brass-inlayer and Brass-founder, Tottenham-mews, Tottenham-street.

Other varieties of specialisation were also beginning to flourish at the time. Small items such as the narrow strips of wood for inlaying were also being made by at least one man, who apparently did nothing else but supply his products to general cabinet-makers. His entry, also in 1825, was abbreviated to fit in the available space, and reads:

> Butler John, Cabinet-stringing-mak[er], 41 George-street, Black-fri[ars]-ro[ad].

The practice increased in the course of the century, so that only the biggest manufacturers found it economical to have departments for each sub-division of their trade. The medium-sized and small makers were able to buy ready-made many of the bits and pieces they required so that a standardisation of the goods produced was the gradual and inevitable result.

THE quantity of surviving 19th-Century furniture is considerably greater than that remaining from the 18th Century. Not only has daily wear and tear been responsible for the loss of so much from the earlier period, but very much more was made in the later to supply the rapidly-rising population. The majority of ordinary pieces of

---

[1] Brian Reade, ibid., pages 253–261.

18th-Century date were worn out long ago, and no record remains of much that was then commonplace. What is extant from the years of Chippendale and Sheraton is, broadly speaking, the best that was made, it has withstood daily usage and changes of fashion, while from 1830 onwards all types and qualities are still represented.

The differences between inexpensive and better furniture are to be seen in the pages of John Claudius Loudon's very popular book, *The Encyclopaedia of Cottage, Farm and Villa Architecture and Furniture*, which was first published in 1833. Loudon, like Henry Holland, had begun his career as a landscape gardener and eventually widened his interests to include architecture and furnishing.[1] An indefatigable worker, in the manner common to many Scotsmen, he died at the age of sixty, sharing the fate of his compatriot, Sir Walter Scott, by writing against time to satisfy his creditors. Mrs. Loudon, herself a writer, penned a short account of her late husband's life,[2] published with his last book in 1845, two years after his death.

Loudon, born in Lanarkshire in 1783, the son of a farmer, came to London at the age of 20 after having gained experience in gardening with two Scottish horticulturalists. Armed with numerous introductions, 'he was soon extensively employed as a landscape-gardener'. He also found time to publish a number of pamphlets, edit two magazines and compile three encyclopaedias. In 1830 he married and in the words of his widow:

In 1832 Mr Loudon commenced his *Encyclopaedia of Cottage, Farm, and Villa Architecture*, which was the first work he ever published on his own account; and in which I was his sole amanuensis, though he had several draughtsmen. The labour that attended his work was immense; and for several months he and I used to sit up the greater part of every night, never having more than four hours' sleep,

Below, *Fig. 156: Another version of 'Pitt's Cabinett Globe Writing Table', also fitted as a sewing-table. The supports are in the form of Atlas. Circa 1810; height 101·6 cm. (Parke-Bernet Galleries, Inc.)*

---

[1] See John Gloag, *Mr. Loudon's England*, Newcastle upon Tyne, 1970.

[2] Reprinted in Gloag, ibid., page 182.

Left, *Fig. 157: Carved oak table, the apron pierced and the legs inset with figures of Wellington, Napoleon and knights of various ages; the top being of porphyry. Circa 1820; width 218·5 cm. (Private collection.)*

Above, *Fig. 158: Table by Henry Whitaker; this and the engraving of the chair in Fig. 154 are dated 1827 although the book in which they were included was published, according to the title-page, in 1825.*

and drinking strong coffee to keep ourselves awake.

The *Encyclopaedia* appeared in 1833, and is a very stout octavo volume some 7 cm. in thickness. Printed in a small but clear type interspersed with numerous neat woodcuts, the 1083 pages are prefaced by 20 of preliminary matter. Apart from the inclusion of some examples of work by a few amateurs, two professionals were responsible for the furniture designs and illustrations.[1] They were W. F. Dalziel[2] and Edward Buckton Lamb. The former was a working cabinet-maker with premises in Little James Street, Bedford Row, which lay just to the north of Holborn. Probably the same man, a William Dalziel had been established from at least 1820 at 24 Great James Street, in the same area. Loudon

credited him with 'nearly all the Designs for modern furniture not specified as having been supplied by other Contributors. These Designs were, for the greater part, drawn by Mr. George Fildes, Professional Draughtsman, 12, Lamb's Conduit Street'.

E. B. Lamb became in due course a well-known architect, and Loudon referred to him as the author of *Etchings of Gothic Ornaments*, which had appeared in six parts in 1830. Earlier, he had been working in

---

[1] See *Loudon's Furniture Designs*, reprinted with an introduction by Christopher Gilbert, 1970.

[2] Heal, op. cit., page 47, notes that the name of William Dalzeel [sic] of 24 Great James Street 'occurs in a correspondence with the Royal Society of Arts which took place in 1817 in connection with mahogany'.

Left, *Fig. 159: Design for a 'Drawing Room Pier Table' by George Smith, 1808.*

Above, *Fig. 160: 'A General View of the Interior of a Drawingroom, fitted up and furnished in the Gothic Style' by Edward Buckton Lamb, from Loudon's* Encyclopaedia, *1833.*

the office of L. N. Cottingham, who restored a number of churches and cathedrals in addition to writing books on medieval architecture.

The principal contributions of Lamb to Loudon's book were designs in the Gothic style, which was making one of its periodic returns to public favour. On this occasion, the Romantic movement apparent in painting and literature, exemplified by Blake's pictures and book-illustrations and by Scott's novels, led the way. Later, John Britton's 14-volume *Cathedral Antiquities of England*, issued between 1814 and 1835, demonstrated the rich variety of ecclesiastical architecture and convinced many that

its splendours should be imitated, if not improved upon, in the home.

The feature likely to strike anyone today looking at Lamb's Gothic is that he apparently aimed unerringly at visual offence and physical discomfort. His 'General View of the Interior of a Drawingroom' (Fig. 160) seems not to have appeared to Loudon otherwise than perfect, for he commented approvingly:

> We need not express an opinion of this interior; for every reader, we think, must be pleased with it. Even the studies of furniture which it affords are interesting; the Gothic piano-forte and music-stool, with the Canterbury on the

left hand, and the music stand on the right; the Gothic couch, with its footstool; the two beautiful chairs; and, finally, the fire-screen, all claim attention, and are each separately worthy of study.

The Gothic library is given an elaborately-beamed roof which it was directed should be partly painted and gilt, and has two chairs and a table in it. The chairs each boast four straight legs, all ornamented; their straightness, although diminishing their stability, being a feature to which Loudon admiringly drew attention:

On examining the chairs, it will be seen that there is not that discrepancy between the hind and the fore legs, that there is in the designs for chairs in the modern style. The backs also of these chairs seem to arise out of the seats, and to be firmly fixed to them, instead of being twisted about in all directions. . . .

Lamb also contributed designs of rooms in the Elizabethan style, which was little less admired at the time than the Gothic, while T. F. Hunt's *Tudor Architecture*, published in 1830, was the source of suitable examples of furniture. Loudon takes the opportunity to warn his readers of the dangers of adapting the style for articles of

Below, *Fig. 161: A Grecian couch, from Loudon's 'Encyclopaedia': 'these couches we consider as handsome articles . . . the curvature of the frame of the head is . . . identical with Hogarth's serpentine line of beauty'.*

Right, *Fig. 162: An 'Astley Cooper's Chair' of beechwood painted and varnished to imitate rosewood.* Circa *1830; height 95·5 cm. (Private collection.)*

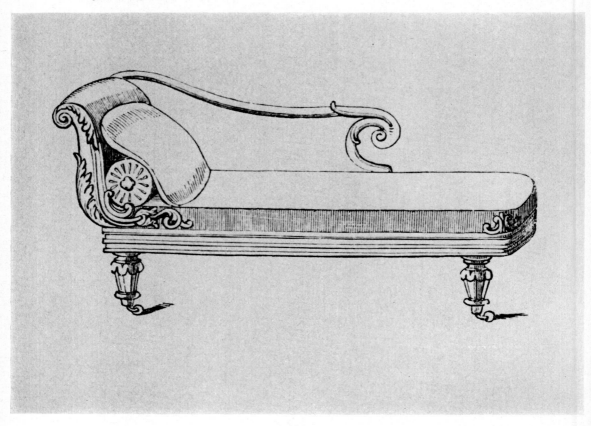

daily use, and it may be wondered why he issued no caution in respect of Gothic. His words have an added interest in the context of the present-day antiques market:

> No one ought to attempt it who is not a master of composition on abstract principles; but indeed (in London, at least), the attempt is scarcely necessary; since there are abundant remains of every kind of Elizabethan furniture to be purchased of collectors. These, when in fragments, are put together, and made up into every article of furniture now in use; and, as London has a direct and cheap communication with every part of the world by sea, the American citizen or the Australian merchant, who wishes to indulge in this taste, may do it with the greatest ease, and may purchase real antiques at much less expense than he could have the articles carved by modern artists.

THE *Encyclopaedia* also contained descriptions and illustrations of 'Grecian and Modern' furniture for cottages and villas which must have been more representative of what was to be seen in homes all over the country. The woodcuts show pieces for every room in a villa from the library to the nursery; the latter including a special chair for children which has often been misdescribed. An example of it is illustrated in Fig. 162, and Loudon wrote of a similar one, stating that it was known as an 'Astley Cooper's chair',

> being a form recommended by that eminent surgeon, with the view of preventing children from acquiring a habit of leaning forward or stooping; the upright position of the back affording support when the child is placed at table, and eating, which a sloping-backed chair does not. It is proper to observe that some medical men do not approve of these chairs.

Possibly the disapproval is reflected in the fact that many such chairs have been sold in modern times as 'Crinoline Chairs', al-

though the small size of the seat is impractical for a grown up whether wearing a crinoline or not.

All the furniture in the section shows a use of Grecian motifs, although in most instances it is clumsily rendered and far removed from Hope's precise imitations. Trusses with drooping acanthus leaves appear on the fronts of sideboards, chiffoniers and Davenports, while alternative patterns have lotus-like petals from which spring columns with leafy capitals. Circular (Loo) tables have carved stems and lions' paw feet beneath quadrangular or triangular bases, and occasional tables are given flat end supports with ribbed baluster stems and spreading legs united by heavy-looking stretchers.

The articles recommended for cottages are simple in appearance and construction

with few concessions to fashion. They include cane-seated chairs, heavy tables, a tall-backed settle and severely practical sofas. The latter, it is suggested, should be raised on castors ('the best castor at present in use is that of Cope of Birmingham'), and covered in strong fabric or given a loose cover of glazed calico. There are also some interesting designs for furniture to be made of cast-iron, which are outside the scope of the present book.

Despite the complimentary remarks of Loudon concerning much of the furniture, he was far from fully approving all he saw. He wrote thus of the great demand for furniture in the capital:

. . . so ardent the desire for novelty, that the great and incessant efforts of

the upholsterer are directed to the production of something new and that this demand for novelty, instead of being met by taste and invention adequate to the supply, has only called forth mechanical changes and combinations of forms.

He was concerned, too, as many since have been, with the taste of the buying

Below, *Fig. 163: Mahogany sideboard inlaid with small panels of satinwood and fitted with gilt metal lion-mask and ring handles. Circa 1820; width 182·8 cm. (Saltram, Devon: The National Trust.)*

public, and with regard to plain or fancy chairs wrote:

> The question is, how far the designer of a chair is justified in deviating from the principle of unity, for the sake of displaying more ornament than he would otherwise be able to show. Ask a cabinet-maker, and he will tell you at once, that his customers prefer the ornamented chair, and care nothing about the unity, or the want of unity, of style. Their great object is to get a display of rich workmanship, at as cheap a rate as possible. Our readers, we are sure, will agree with us, that this taste on the part of the purchaser is of a vulgar and grovelling kind, and ought to be corrected. This can only be done by enlightening the minds of the public in general on the subject of taste; and this is one of the grand objects of our work.

The *Encyclopaedia* was issued again in 1839 with the title-page containing the words: 'A New Edition, with numerous corrections, and with many of the plates re-engraved'. The principal change, however, lay in the replacement by woodcuts of the 'nearly one hundred lithographs' of the

Below, *Fig. 164: Four-part table made of mahogany. The end supports are 'X'-shaped with a central floral motif. Circa 1825; overall length 247 cm. (Private collection.)*

first edition. The number of pages is the same in both instances, and locating the 'numerous corrections' is akin to seeking the elusive needle in a haystack.

A supplement to the *Encyclopaedia* was issued in 1842, in 1846 Mrs. Loudon edited the whole work and it was printed under the slightly shortened title *Cottage, Farm and Villa Architecture and Furniture.* Further editions appeared until as late as 1867, the book having then been available continuously for a period of 34 years since it had first been put on the market. The author of it pointed out that its success depended on 'the spirit of observation and inquiry which it excites in the general reader', and there can be little doubt that it had a considerable effect during its long currency.

Below, *Fig 165: Mahogany wine table on reeded supports, the two ends hinge to fold downwards and there is a shaped piece to fill the central gap and convert the article into a side table. Circa 1810; width 151 cm. (John Keil, Ltd.) Loudon writes of a similar, but later, article: 'It is chiefly used by gentlemen after the ladies have retired to the drawing room. This table is then placed in front of the fire, with its convex side outwards, and the guests sit round that side, with their feet to the fire.'* **Right,** *Plate 26: Rosewood work table with silk-covered bag. Circa 1835; width 76·8 cm. (Saltram, Devon: The National Trust.)*

14 : Early Victorian

THE period between 1840 and 1850 was one when design was in a state of flux. Numerous styles were in common use and appeared, more often than not, in company

Left, *Fig. 166:* '*Illustration of the extravagant style of Modern Gothic Furniture and Decoration*', from *A. W. N. Pugin's* The True Principles of Pointed or Christian Architecture, *1841.* **Below,** *Fig. 167: Brass cot, 'the figure of a guardian angel at the head supports the curtain', exhibited in 1851 by R. W. Winfield of Birmingham.*

with one another. J. C. Loudon wrote in his *Encyclopaedia* of the state of affairs in the year 1833, or just prior, but he did not alter his words for the 'New Edition' of six years later. It may be assumed, therefore, that they still applied:

> The principal Styles of Design in Furniture, as at present executed in Britain, may be reduced to four; viz., the Grecian or modern style, which is by far the most prevalent; the Gothic or perpendicular style, which imitates the lines and angles of the Tudor Gothic Architecture; the Elizabethan style, which combines the Gothic with the Roman or Italian manner; and the style of the age of Louis XIV., or the florid Italian, which is characterised by curved lines and excess of curvilinear ornaments. The first or modern style is by far the most general, and the second has been more or less the fashion in Gothic houses from the commencement of the present century; since which period the third and fourth are occasionally to be met with, and the demand for them is rather on the increase than otherwise.

From the foregoing it would seem that the furniture made in the period being discussed left a choice of style entirely to the taste of the buyer, who could select whichever his fancy or his education dictated. It has been mentioned that the taste of the early Victorian period was notably con-

servative, and the length of time during which Loudon's book remained in print, little altered, confirms the suggestion. Equally, Thomas King's *The Modern Style of Cabinet Work Exemplified*, was available for just as long a term of years, having been first published in 1829 and considered to be worthy of re-issue, unaltered in its contents, in 1862.[1] The state of affairs was appreciated at the time, and steps were duly taken by a few of the more far-sighted men to stimulate designers into being more forward-looking.

The pendulum of Romanticism had swung widely, as pendulums of fashion invariably do, and from its beginning in the late 18th Century, the movement had by 1840 reached a stage of sentimentally aping the distant past. Scott had fired the general public with his novels, and his building of Abbotsford, Roxburghshire, in 1822-3, in full-blooded Gothic, proved to one and all that his heart lay in his work. Research, careful and otherwise, was directed to the Age of Chivalry, and men like Sir Samuel Rush Meyrick, a lawyer, set about acquiring and publishing knowledge of arms and armour. He helped to arrange the big collections at Windsor Castle and in the Tower of London, formed a big collection himself and in 1824 wrote a history of the subject. As a result of Sir Samuel's assistance, Henry Shaw, an antiquary and illuminator, published a book of engravings entitled *Specimens of Ancient Furniture* in 1836. The original drawings were the work of Meyrick William Twopeny, Shaw himself and others, and the 74 plates show a range of objects from frames to bedsteads. In the light of subsequent knowledge the illustrations do not all match up to the wording of their captions, but Sir Samuel, who wrote the brief

commentary on each item, was careful to commit himself only occasionally on their countries of origin. Thus, some ebony chairs are noted as being of the reign of Charles II and presumably English, but they are of a type that remains common today and are now known to have been made in the East Indies. Again, an ivory salt cellar is 'probably Danish or Icelandic', but modern scholarship names it more plausibly but still without absolute precision, as 'Afro-Portugese'.[2]

A few years earlier, the architect T. F. Hunt, who was Clerk of the Works at Whitehall and elsewhere, wrote his *Exemplars of Tudor Architecture . . . and Observations on the Furniture of the Tudor Period*, which was issued in 1830. Of the 193 pages of text in the volume, 102 were devoted to architecture and the remainder to 'Furniture, &c.', while some of the few plates illustrating the subject depict the same examples as Shaw used 6 years later.

Watercolour artists were also active in propagating knowledge of former centuries. John Buckler was at work drawing and engraving ancient churches and secular buildings, while Joseph Nash, who is not to be confused with the architect, John Nash, made an extensive series of watercolours which were printed by lithography and published between 1839 and 1849. Nash's *The Mansions of England in the Olden Time* totalled a hundred plates which were issued in four separate series, showing the houses, in the words of the artist, 'enlivened with the presence of their inmates and guests'.

From these men and numerous others, the public did not lack entertainment and

---

[1] Peter Floud, 'Furniture', in *The Connoisseur's Period Guides: The Early Victorian Period*, 1958, page 1319.

[2] W. P. Fagg, *Afro-Portuguese Ivories*, no date, plates 7-11. The salt cellar, which belonged in 1836 to Sir Samuel Rush Meyrick, was presented to the British Museum in 1878.

Left, *Fig. 168: Mahogany writing cabinet carved in the Rococo style. Circa 1850; Width 173 cm. (H. Blairman & Sons.)*

Above, *Fig. 169: 'Brass four-post Bedstead, in the Renaissance Style, clothed in Green Silk Damask', shown at the Great Exhibition of 1851 by R. W. Winfield.*

education, but the style of furnishing, admired as it was in a stately home, was not to every taste when adapted in scale and content for use in suburban dwellings. More attractive in such a setting was the 'Grecian or modern', which was a watered-down version of Thomas Hope with the addition of carved or other features. The even more modern French-inspired style, which Loudon indicated was gaining in popularity, was known under several names, most of them inappropriate, and was described by contemporaries of his as 'Louis XIV, Louis XV, Rococo, Old French, or even the "florid Italian"'.[1]

The only furniture of the time that was being executed with definite ideas in the mind of its designer was in the pure Gothic style evolved by Augustus Welby Northmore Pugin. He was the son of an architectural draughtsman who came to England from France in 1793, and was employed by architects as well as making drawings on his own account. In his works on Gothic buildings[2] he was assisted by his son, in whom was aroused an interest in the style that developed quickly over the years.

A. W. N. Pugin was employed in 1827 to design some furniture for Windsor Castle,

[1] Elizabeth Aslin, *19th Century English Furniture,* 1962, page 30.

[2] A. C. Pugin, *Specimens of Gothic Architecture* 1821–3, and *Gothic Ornaments from Ancient Buildings in England and France,* 1831.

which he later criticised strongly on the grounds that 'although the parts were correct and exceedingly well executed, collectively they appeared a complete burlesque of pointed design'. His furniture, however, was only a portion of his artistic activity, which was principally devoted to buildings; above all, to providing the details for Sir Charles Barry's Houses of Parliament, erected between the years 1840 and 1860 to replace the building destroyed by fire in 1834. Pugin's life was an unsettled one: his first wife died in childbirth, his second marriage was followed by his conversion to Roman Catholicism, and three years after his third marriage, which took place in 1849, he became insane and died.

His piety and his Gothic were not accepted by all, and one critic wrote of him:

. . . with the assumed conviction that the Romish Church is the only one by which the grand and sublime style of ecclesiastical architecture can be re-

Below, *Fig. 170: Rosewood occasional table with gilt metal mounts and an inlaid marble top. Circa 1830; width 102·9 cm. (Saltram, Devon: The National Trust.)*

Right, *Fig. 171: Marble-topped cabinet japanned, painted and gilt in the style of papier-mâché. Circa 1850; width about 60 cm. (Mallett & Son, Ltd.)*

Above, *Fig. 172: Rosewood piano-chair the seat adjustable for height.* Circa *1840; minimum height 81·3 cm. (J. K. des Fontaines, Esq., F.R.S.A.)*

Other men's Gothic was little more than Grecian with a few added cusps and crockets, but this did not satisfy Pugin. He wrote about it with his customary vigour:

> . . . your modern man designs a sofa or occasional table from details culled out of Britton's Cathedrals, and all the ordinary articles of furniture, which require to be simple and convenient, are made not only very expensive but very uneasy. We find diminutive flying buttresses about an armchair; every thing is crocketed with angular projections, innumerable mitres, sharp ornaments, and turreted extremities. A man who remains any length of time in a modern Gothic room, and escapes without being wounded by some of its minutiae, may consider himself extremely fortunate. There are often as many pinnacles and gablets about a pier-glass frame as are to be found in an ordinary church, and not unfrequently the whole canopy of a tomb has been transferred for the purpose, as at Strawberry Hill.[2]

To back this argument he appended an illustration (Fig. 166) which may be compared with E. B. Lamb's Gothic drawing room shown on page 201.

In spite of Pugin's careful research, the public did not pay his words much attention, and his furniture was for the few rather than for the many. His writings were addressed to his fellow-architects rather than to those setting-up a home, and his influence in his lifetime was greater in the building world than in the cabinet-maker's workshop.

vived, he quitted the Protestant faith, which was possibly never very strong with him, and entered the Romish Church.[1]

He built a number of churches for those of his adopted faith, and spent the years subsequent to his conversion convincing the world of the rightness of his opinions.

Pugin did for Gothic much the same as Thomas Hope had done earlier for Grecian: both went back to the originators of the styles and aimed to re-create their work with exactitude. They attempted, with some success, to reproduce the past, if not to improve on it, by investigating the principles behind the designs employed.

F URNITURE of the years 1840–50 is almost exclusively made of oak, walnut or mahogany and, less often, rosewood. The exotic timbers seen at the beginning of the

---

[1] Samuel Redgrave, op. cit., page 343.

[2] *The True Principles of Pointed or Christian Architecture*, page 35.

century, such as zebra-wood, calamander, satinwood and thuya were rarely employed, and inlays of either wood or metal seldom appeared. At the same time, brass handles fell from favour and simple turned wood knobs were used. This last is a fashion that has provoked argument, the theory being put forward that metal handles were stripped and replaced with wood at an earlier date in order to finance the war against Napoleon.

The majority of articles that had proved their daily usefulness continued to be made. The smaller dining rooms made do with a chiffonier, a low cabinet with a shallow shelf or two above the top, but large houses had versions of the earlier pedestal sideboard with Grecian or French ornament superimposed. The backboard of the latter grew taller, and in place of polished wood was filled with panels of mirror glass.[1]

The 1840's saw the use of furniture constructed wholly or in part of papier-mâché; a material originating in the Far East, and revived by the French who introduced it into England in the later 18th Century. The most renowned maker of it was Henry Clay, of Birmingham, who patented his process in 1772. He made his ware by glueing together sheets of unsized porous paper and the resulting card-like material was shaped in a mould and dried. It could be cut with a saw and planed in the same manner as wood, and was finished by applying coats of paints and varnishes to be hardened in heat.

Clay grew rich from his invention, and part of this was doubtless due to his own personality. Like Josiah Wedgwood, he was alive to the value of Royal patronage, and is said to have supplied Queen Charlotte with a papier-mâché sedan chair, or at least one with paper panels, as well as with other articles. On his retirement in 1802 he

Above, *Fig. 173: Carved mahogany hall chair, the back in the form of a shell. Circa 1830; height 91·5 cm. (J. K. des Fontaines, Esq., F.R.S.A.)*

had been appointed 'Japanner in Ordinary' to George III and the Prince of Wales, and was alleged to have more than 600 employees.

The majority of extant papier-mâché dates from the 19th Century, in the first half of which the firm of Jennens and Bettridge, also of Birmingham, was preeminent. Much of the output, like that of their competitors in the same city and in nearby Wolverhampton, comprised tea trays, snuff boxes, coasters and other small-sized articles for which the material was eminently suitable. Most of them were given a black japanned surface, but green, red and other colours were sometimes used

---

[1] Peter Floud, op. cit., pages 1324–30.

and all were decorated skilfully in colours and gold. From about 1825 an innovation appeared in the employment of thin pieces of mother-of-pearl inset in the ground and painted over with transparent tints. The shell was occasionally used with ingenuity to give moonlight effects, but more often than not it formed the petals of flowers to which it adds a slight lustre.

A few manufacturers, including Jennens and Bettridge, whose work was often stamped with their name, produced pieces of furniture in papier-mâché. Tables, chairs and pole fire-screens would appear to have been the most popular articles, but ambition did not cease with equipping the drawing room, and a complete bedroom suite is to be seen at Temple Newsam House, Leeds. The dressing table from the suite, which includes a bedstead, is shown in Plate 29 on page 226.

Typical of the chairs of *circa* 1845–50 are the two in Fig. 175. Although they are identical in shape, with pierced curved

Left, *Fig. 174: Wooden chair, japanned and decorated in imitation of papier-mâché. Circa 1850. (Private collection.)*

Below, *Fig. 175: Two papier-mâché chairs decorated with mother-of-pearl, painting and gilding. Circa 1845. (Private collection.)*

backs and sharp-edged cabriole legs, their decoration varies: the right-hand one bearing butterflies with mother-of-pearl wings. Both chairs have loose upholstered seats, but in most instances the seats are caned. The fashion for such chairs inspired imitations in the form of wooden ones coated with black composition similarly ornamented with pearl, painting and gilding (Fig. 174).

At the same date further uses for the material were advocated by Charles

Below, Fig. 176: Armchair with barley-twist turned legs and back supports, upholstered in brightly coloured gros-point needlework. Circa 1845; height 72 cm. (Private collection.)

Right, Fig. 177: Invalid chair with a carved mahogany frame, the wheels actuated by turning the handles on the arms. Circa 1830. (Mallett & Sons, Ltd.)

Frederick Bielefeld, who had a showroom in Wellington Street, Strand, and published a large volume publicising his goods.[1] Mostly they were for architectural use, such as cornice and ceiling ornaments, but he further proposed their application

> to the enriched scroll legs of cabinets and pier-tables, in the old French style; to ornamental brackets for clocks, busts, vases, &c. . . . also . . . to the canopies of bedsteads, &c. &c. It has been very advantageously used for the latter purpose in the state-bed at Chatsworth; and also to the canopy of the Royal Throne in the present house of Lords.

Earlier, a comparable use had been made of papier-mâché, when it sometimes formed the frames of mirrors. More ambitious was its employment by the architect, John Nash, for roofing Caerhays Castle, Cornwall, when he rebuilt the mansion in 1808. The result might have been foreseen, as was reported by someone at a slightly later date:

> The plain old-fashioned place of the Trevanions was replaced by a most inappropriate castellated mansion, which, having been erected by Nash, who thought more of plan than of execution, was absurdly roofed with papier mâché, a new invention of the day, which Mr. Nash was certainly not justified in recommending to an inexperienced young man in a county so proverbially wet as Cornwall. The consequence was that when this roof, cracked by the sun and penetrated by wet, ceased to protect the interior, there were no means of mending it, and after assisting to choose the site, I lived to see the new house a desolate ruin for many years, after the no less striking ruin of the family.[2]

As an alternative to papier-mâché for those seeking variety, there was furniture made of metal. This had been recommended by Loudon in 1833, and later, as suitable for cottages and public houses, where daily wear and tear might be hard. He showed designs in the shape of chairs and tables, some of the former being made

from lengths of gas piping incorporating a cast iron seat and back. Others are entirely of cast iron, but of one he warns the reader: 'if roughly used, it might be liable to fracture, but it would form an excellent chair for the entrance hall of an inn, or even of a villa'. The tables included patterns for cast-iron end supports, of a type which remains in use, and which Loudon wrote were then to be seen in the Albion Tavern, Drury Lane Theatre. While the tables are acceptable for such use, the idea of employing metal furniture in the home must have had a very limited appeal, for none of it seems to have survived. There are to be found, however, cast-iron garden chairs and seats, for which metal is a more suitable material than good mahogany. In the 1840's a more determined effort was made to supplant wood with metal, and the Coalbrookdale Ironworks, in Shropshire, was prominent among those who entered the market. Upholstered chairs and other articles for living rooms were made but, likewise, all appear to have vanished long ago, for which we may be thankful.

Less unpleasant to contemplate are iron bedsteads which, with or without tall posts, began to appear in about 1830. At the same date, beds made of brass were available, but did not catch the public imagination until the late 1840's. By 1851 they could be purchased in several of the prevailing styles, including the Renaissance which is illustrated in Fig. 169.

---

[1] C. F. Bielefeld, *On the Use of the Improved Papier-Mâché in Furniture, in the Interior Decoration of Buildings, and in Works of Art*, undated, but probably issued in about 1843. Copies differ in their contents, the number of plates varying between 120 and 140, plus a frontispiece.

[2] Christine Hawkridge, 'Sarah Gregor of Trewarthenick', in *Journal of the Royal Institution of Cornwall*, New Series, Vol. VI, part I (1969), page 20.

Fig 2.

Fig 3.

Fig 5

Fig 6

3 Feet.

15 : Mid-Victorian

*Left, Fig. 178: 'National Emblem Chairs', see Fig. 180.
Below, Fig. 179: Armchair carved in bog-yew by J. A. Jones
of Dublin and shown in the 1851 exhibition. Wood-cut from
the Art-Journal Illustrated Catalogue.*

THE mid-Victorian years opened and were dominated by the Great Exhibition of 1851. It lived up to its name, both at the time and in subsequent years during which its success has become legendary. One of the tangible sequels to the occasion is the Victoria and Albert Museum, founded as the 'Museum of Ornamental Art' as the result of a grant of £5,000 from the Treasury for the purchase of articles from the Exhibition. Between 1899 and 1909, on land purchased out of the proceeds of the same Exhibition, the present building was erected, and from the original conception of demonstrating the 'application of fine art to objects of utility' it has become a world-famous repository of works of art.

In 1842 the Prince Consort became President of the Society of Arts, which had been founded nearly a century earlier and was fast becoming outdated in its ideas. Two years later, the French held the tenth in a series of Exhibitions of their own products; a display that had been initiated in 1797 by a small 3-day show held in a building erected on the Champ de Mars, Paris. The 1844 *Exposition* showed selected examples of the work of nearly 4,000 manufacturers of all kinds of goods and took place in the Champs Elysées. Its success induced the Society of Arts to attempt something similar in London, but English manufacturers proved indifferent to the project and it was dropped. In its place the Society offered prizes 'for a series of Models

and Designs of useful objects, calculated to improve general taste'.

Once again there was little response, but among the articles submitted was a teaset designed by 'Felix Summerly' and made by Mintons of Stoke-on-Trent. The pseudonym was that of Mr. (later, Sir) Henry Cole, an energetic public official then in his early thirties. He started a small firm, which was named 'Felix Summerly Manufactures', to commission designs from selected artists, and the designs were then sold to makers who paid a royalty on sales to Summerly's. Cole attended to publicity, but after a few years the business was closed.

In 1847 the prizewinners and a few others participated in an exhibition held by the Society. It was seen by 29,000 members of the public and it was decided to repeat the experiment in the next year. As this proved even more successful than the first, it was proposed to hold such shows in each succeeding year with a special quinquennial exhibition in 1851.

As it turned out, the Prince took the reins, and early in 1849 he stated:

> Now is the time to prepare for a Great Exhibition—an Exhibition worthy of the greatness of this country; not merely national in its scope and benefits, but comprehensive of the whole world; and I offer myself to the public as their leader, if they are willing to assist in the undertaking.

Henry Cole was involved in the project from its inception, and while on a visit to Buckingham Palace in connection with the preliminary details he discussed with Prince Albert the important subject of a suitable site. The latter suggested Leicester Square, but Cole thought it would prove too small

and in reply to a query proposed Hyde Park, which was duly accepted.

The Exhibition was opened by Queen Victoria, accompanied by her Consort on the 1st May 1851, in a vast building designed by Sir Joseph Paxton and constructed mainly of cast-iron and glass. Not for nothing had Paxton been in charge of the gardens and greenhouses at Chatsworth; his Hyde Park building was no more than an enormous conservatory and quickly earned the name, 'The Crystal Palace'. From the day it opened until it closed on 11th October of the same year it was visited by 6,039,195 people, and the final accounts showed that it had gained for the Commissioners, who had been responsible for organising and running it, a profit of £186,437. The number of individual articles displayed totalled more than 100,000 shown by 13,937 exhibitors, of whom the British Isles and Empire accounted for 7,381 and other nations 6,556.[1]

The many English companies and individuals who showed furniture in 1851 were grouped in Class 26, which comprised also upholstery, paper hangings, papier-mâché and japanned articles. The quantity alone makes it difficult to judge in retrospect, but it has also to be remembered that there was international competition, and national as well as local reputations were at stake.

Inevitably, later attention has focused on the 'freaks' that were shown in each class, but on examination they prove to have been only a small proportion of the whole. In addition, the numerous woodcut illustrations published at the time give

---

[1] John Timbs, *The Year-Book of Facts in The Great Exhibition of 1851*, 1851; Sir Henry Trueman Wood, *The History of the Royal Society of Arts*, 1913; C. H. Gibbs-Smith. *The Great Exhibition of 1851*, 1950.

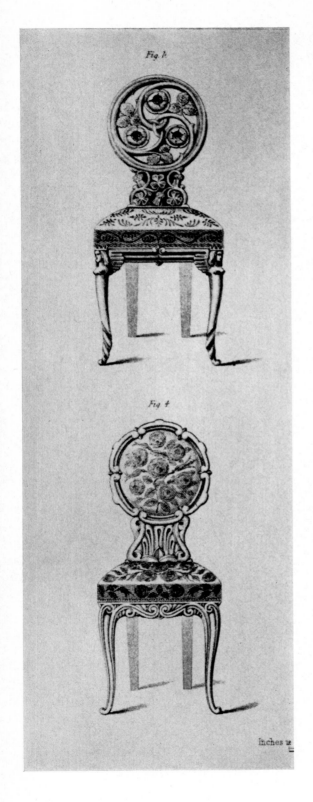

Fig. 1

Fig. 4

inches 12

an inadequate idea of the originals. Twentieth-Century readers are used to renderings by photography, and the very different appearance of drawings reproduced by wood-blocks requires an adjustment of vision often difficult to achieve.

The exhibits were judged by a number of juries composed of experts in each craft and drawn from many countries. The twelve men dealing with Class 26 were under the chairmanship of Professor Roesner, of Austria, who was President of the Imperial Academy of Fine Arts, the deputy-chairman being Lord Ashburton, and the remaining ten members included five from England, so that British and Foreign representatives were equal in number. The jury voted on the merits of each article, and listed their awards of medals and 'Honourable Mentions'.

The jury in question prefaced their report by noting that furnishings in general employed much skilled labour and were a clue to the state of industrial art in the various countries. The report then makes a number of telling remarks, which show that the jury was aware of deficiencies in the exhibits, both individually and collectively; deficiencies often thought to have passed unnoticed at the time and to have been observed only by the more perceptive eyes of later critics. The remarks applying to furniture were brief and to the point:

It is important, both for the strength and good effect of furniture, that the principles of sound construction be well carried out, that the construction be evident, and that if carving or other ornament be introduced, it should be by decorating that construction itself, not by overlaying and disguising it.

It is not necessary that an object be covered with ornament, or be extravagant in form, to obtain the element of beauty; articles of furniture are too often crowded with unnecessary embellishment, which, besides adding to their cost, interferes with their use, purpose, and convenience; the perfection of art manufacture consists in combining, with the greatest possible effect, the useful with the pleasing, and the execution of this can generally be most successfully carried out by adopting the simplest process.[1]

The jury then expressed their regret 'that there had not been more specimens of ordinary furniture for general use'; which is a criticism invariably associated with public displays. The bigger and more important the occasion, the more probable it is that everyday objects will be excluded in favour of those deemed likely to gain prestige for the maker. This was certainly the case in 1851, when the carver's chisel so frequently ran riot, and nation rivalled nation in the production of eye-catching exhibits.

The pieces most clearly illustrating the jury's comments were a number forming a suite made from Irish bog-yew, wood seasoned and coloured by lengthy immersion in wet soil, which was exhibited by

---

[1] *Reports by the Juries*, 1852.

Left, *Fig. 180: 'National Emblem Chairs' furnish a striking example of how much originality may be produced from the most familiar objects, when treated in a true artistic spirit.*

Below, *Fig. 181: 'Ladies Work Tables' for execution in various woods. This and Figs. 178 and 180 are from* The Cabinet-Maker's Assistant, *1863.* (*Dover reprint, 1970.*)

A. J. Jones of Dublin. The whole was 'designed to illustrate the history, antiquities, animal and vegetable productions, &c., of Ireland'. The armchair illustrated in Fig. 179 was described thus:

> Chivalric bustos of ancient Irish warriors form the outline of the back, and the ancient arms of Ireland, as given on the authority of Sir William Betham, Bart., are in the centre. The elbows of the chair formed by wolf dogs —one at ease and recumbent, with the motto on the collar, 'Gentle when stroked'; the other irritated, with the counter motto, 'Fierce when provoked'.[1]

Jones of Dublin was only one of the many who displayed their skill at intricate carving. A few years earlier there had been a vogue for such work by amateurs, who were encouraged by the award of prizes. These were given by the Society of Arts at the suggestion of the Prince Consort, no doubt recalling the triumphs of German woodcarvers in the past. A School of Art Wood-

Above, *Fig. 182: The 'Kenilworth' sideboard, carved by Cookes and Son of Warwick from an oak grown at Kenilworth, Warwickshire. It depicts scenes from Sir Walter Scott's novel* Kenilworth. *An engraving after a daguerrotype from Tallis's* The Great Exhibition Illustrated.

carving was eventually set up in the Albert Hall, in 1880 an exhibition of old and modern work was held there, and 'by the nineties everyone who felt the need of a genteel and improving pastime, from the Princess of Wales to the humblest clerk, did a little chip-carving'.[2]

There was, however, nothing amateur about the earnest band of carvers centred on Warwick: J. M. Willcox, the Kendalls, and William Cookes. The latter made the Kenilworth sideboard (Fig. 182), amongst others, a *tour-de-force* at the sight of which

---

[1] *Official Descriptive and Illustrated Catalogue*, 3 vols., 1851, vol. II, pages 735–9. A fourth, supplementary, volume was published in 1853.

[2] Elizabeth Aslin, op. cit., page 52.

Above, *Fig. 183: Ebonised beechwood settee with a rush seat. This type was supplied by Morris, Marshall, Faulkner & Co., from about 1865.*

one can do no more than echo the words of a writer in the *Art-Journal* catalogue: 'any attempt to describe this elaborately carved piece of workmanship would, in our limited space, be out of the question'.[1] The skill of such men, and those in London and other provincial centres, was not limited to the dining room, but was later let loose in the chancel. There, many plain church interiors were duly embellished with intricately patterned oak screens and stalls, replacing those of earlier centuries made by craftsmen whose labour had been equally painstaking but usually with more artistic and appropriate results.

The inlaid wood work, known popularly as Tunbridge Wells Ware, was a product of the Kentish town, where it had been made in one variety or another from at least the early 18th Century.[2] Examples shown in 1851 included what was called the 'Chromatrope Table', which was said by its exhibitor, Edmund Nye, to display a mosaic of 129,500 pieces of English and foreign woods in their natural colours. A work cabinet made by Nye, and the label beneath its base are illustrated in Figs. 184 and 185.

There was plenty in the Crystal Palace at which to marvel, but all too little in the way of furniture for the average home. The remedy appeared a couple of years later when the anonymously compiled *Cabinet-Maker's Assistant* was published.[3] The 101

---

[1] *The Art-Journal Illustrated Catalogue of the Exhibition of the Industry of All Nations*, no date but c. 1851.

[2] E. H. & E. R. Pinto, *Tunbridge and Scottish Souvenir Woodware*, 1970.

[3] The third edition (1863) reprinted with an introduction by John Gloag, as *The Victorian Cabinet-Maker's Assistant*, London and New York, 1970.

plates in it are mostly versions of the exhibits seen in Hyde Park, the writer of the Preface stating:

> They include an extensive range, from the most simple to the most elaborate in style; and are thus fitted to serve as models for furniture for the houses of all grades of the middle and upper classes of the community.

He also wrote of the difficulty of obtaining 'good and novel designs', and having acquired them, he added, somewhat surprisingly,

> they may, in fact, be multiplied indefinitely by engrafting the decorations of one on the form of another. . . .

Thus, the craftsman was encouraged to ring the changes and convert a pattern from Grecian to Elizabethan with nothing more than the touch of a chisel. Many took the advice rather than heed the measured words of the 1851 jury. Whether the makers were to blame for the quantity of poorly-designed pieces turned out, or whether they had no option but to fill an untutored public demand is a debatable point. Certainly there survives a depressingly large amount of such furniture, but when time has weeded out the worst it may be easier to form a clear judgement of the achievements of the cabinet-makers of the time.

At about the date of the Exhibition a group of young painters had decided on a fresh approach to their art and named themselves the 'Pre-Raphaelite Brother-

Below, *Fig. 184: Work-cabinet decorated with Tunbridge Wells mosaic and veneered with walnut, made by Edmund Nye. Circa 1850; width 19 cm. (Mrs. U. des Fontaines.)*

hood'; their objective being to model their style on that current in the days before Raphael. It has been said that 'the course of English art changed radically in 1850, largely through the influence of Rossetti, Millais and Holman Hunt . . . with some help from Ford Madox Brown'.[1] They were championed by John Ruskin while being denounced by Charles Dickens, and became the focus for all who professed an interest in progressive art and a possibility of a change for the better.

The Brotherhood aroused keen interest at the universities, and in 1853, when William Morris went into residence at Exeter College, Oxford, he quickly found

himself a place among some 'advanced thinkers' who were imitatively named the Brotherhood. Morris, a young man from a well-to-do family, had intended entering the Church, but before long came to the conclusion that he could be of more service to mankind as a layman. Within a few years Morris had passed his finals and entered an architect's office. He did not stay there long, for he met and became friendly with Dante Gabriel Rossetti, who persuaded him that he would be better employed as a painter than as an architect.

[1] Graham Reynolds, *Victorian Painting*, 1966, page 60.

Below, *Fig. 185: Edmund Nye's printed label beneath the cabinet in Fig. 184.*

In 1859 William Morris married, and in the same year began building a house, Upton, Bexleyheath, Kent, designed for him by Philip Webb. He studiously supervised every detail, both external and internal, and a couple of years later decided that the public might benefit from his experience. He founded the firm of Morris, Marshall, Faulkner & Company, with premises at 8 Red Lion Square, London, whose prospectus stated they would decorate churches and homes, provide designs for and supply stained glass, metalwork and wallpapers, as well as fabrics and carpets, and carving.

The partners in the venture included Rossetti, the painters Burne-Jones and Madox Brown, and Philip Webb. Although it is popularly thought that Morris himself designed furniture for the firm, this is not so. He is said to have made a table while he was at Oxford to prove he was 'a practical man',[1] but did not pursue the activity.

---

[1] Elizabeth Aslin, op. cit., page 57.

Left, *Fig. 186: Decorated oak writing cabinet designed by the architect, Richard Norman Shaw in about 1860. Width 142 cm. (Sotheby's.)*

Below, *Fig. 187: Table with the octagonal top and base veneered with ebony inlaid with ivory, mother-of-pearl and stained woods. Circa 1840; width 152·4 cm. (Christie's.)*

Ford Madox Brown and Holman actually did design furniture, and it was some of their work as well as adapted traditional-style pieces that made the firm widely known and ensured its profits (Fig. 183).

In 1862 a further international Exhibition was held in London, and again about 6,000,000 saw it. Morris and Co. showed a few items, including stained glass windows, tapestries and 'Decorated Furniture'. The last, although appreciated only by the few, had a growing influence as the years passed.

They were pieces of simple form but well made and decorated with paintings, usually by one or other of the Brotherhood, and which one contemporary critic suggested should be framed and the rest burned.[1]

Morris and his partners were not alone in their endeavours to influence and improve

---

[1] Elizabeth Aslin, op. cit., page 57.

Below, *Fig. 188: Two upholstered arm-chairs with carved rosewood arms and legs. Circa 1850. (Lanhydrock, Cornwall: The National Trust.)*

Right, *Fig. 189: Walnut chair with carved 'balloon' back and cabriole legs. Circa 1850; height 90 cm. (J. K. des Fontaines, Esq., F.R.S.A.)*

furniture design. Two architects in particular, Norman Shaw and William Burges, also played a part, designing cabinets and other pieces which relied on painting for much of their effect. Norman Shaw's writing-table and cabinet in Fig. 187 was made shortly before 1862, and betrays the hand of a man more used to working on buildings than on their contents. Burges produced similar pieces in a heavy pseudo-medieval style. His cabinet in the Victoria and Albert Museum[1] is painted all over, the front with a central panel by E. J. Poynter depicting an armoured combat entitled 'The Battle between Wines and Beers', with flanking portraits of men and women who look as out of place as the donors on a 15th-Century triptych. Like much earlier furniture, it is perhaps less than fair to judge it when it is removed from the surroundings for which it was originally designed.

[1] Elizabeth Aslin, op. cit., plate 60.

Below, *Fig. 190: Walnut music Canterbury with fretted divisions, a drawer in the base and porcelain castors below short turned legs. Circa 1850: width 59·7 cm. (Lanhydrock, Cornwall: The National Trust.)*

Right, *Plate 30: Walnut chair with 'balloon' back and cabriole legs. Circa 1850; height 87 cm. (Private collection.)*

16 : Late Victorian

IN the later 1860's there were two distinct styles of furnishing jostling for acceptance: the ornate which followed on from the 1851 Exhibition show-pieces, and the

Left, *Fig. 191: 'A comfortable corner', woodcut illustration to* The Drawing Room, *by Mrs. Orrinsmith, published in 1878.* **Below, Fig. 192:** *Carved mahogany armchair dated 1864, based on a design by A. W. N. Pugin of about 1840. Height 111·7 cm. (Temple Newsam House, Yorkshire: Leeds City Art Gallery.)*

simpler pseudo-medieval stemming from Pugin and the Gothicists. The spirit of Pugin himself remained strong, and as late as 1864, a dozen years after his death, one of his early designs was the inspiration for the armchair shown in Fig. 192. Less obviously, his Gothic began to appear in furniture made by the bigger manufacturers, to whom it had come by way of Morris and his school. The large sideboard in Fig. 194, resembling nothing so much as an altar and reredos, was exhibited at the 1867 Paris International Exhibition by one of the prominent London makers, Holland and Sons, of Mount Street.

A propagandist for simple lines in furniture was Charles Locke Eastlake, who was vehemently opposed to the 'intemperate use of curves'. Eastlake was keeper and secretary of the National Gallery between 1878 and 1898, and is frequently confused with his relative and near-namesake, Sir Charles Lock Eastlake, P.R.A., whose career included a term as director of the same gallery. The former lived until 1906, and his writings included *Hints on Household Taste*, which was first published in 1868 and was a 'best seller' in its class.

In his book, C. L. Eastlake illustrated some pieces of his own design which he considered to be improvements on those of others. His sideboard, for instance, is a clumsy-looking rectangular piece with a

superstructure of open shelves topped by a motto in Latin: this last a feature of a proportion of the furniture made from then onwards, when suitable admonitions, sometimes in English, were incised or painted over beds, mantels and elsewhere. His views on furniture include use of the word 'picturesque' as an alternative to the more commonplace 'art' or 'artistic', which were equivalent to the present-day usage of 'contemporary'. Eastlake railed against 'the practice which exists of encircling toilet-tables with a sort of muslin petticoat generally stiffened by a crinoline of pink or blue calico'. In its stead he proposed a severely unfeminine alternative (Fig. 193), with what appears to be machine-carved ornament on the supports of the looking-glass, which, he wrote, 'may give a picturesque character to such articles of furniture'.

Mechanical carving was not unknown in 1851, but little use was made of it and there were few signs of it at the Exhibition. Steam power began to be employed in big workshops soon after this date, but was applied mainly to sawing and moulding. Powered carving was executed by means of a series of drills, but doubtless required finishing by hand and was reckoned to be uneconomic. Once the public would accept it as it left the machine, after the latter had been improved, it became a profitable operation. Eastlake was not silent on the matter:

> It may be laid down as a general rule, that wherever wood-carving is introduced in the design of second-rate furniture it is egregiously and utterly bad. It is frequently employed in the most inappropriate places—it is generally spiritless in design, and always worthless in execution.[1]

His remarks were directed against ready-carved mouldings and small ornaments to be applied to frames and consoles, but he makes no mention of other carving being performed mechanically.

Left, *Plate 31: Carved oak sideboard. Circa 1870; width 214 cm. (Private collection.)* **Above,** *Fig. 193: Toilet table made by Jackson and Graham to a design by Charles Locke Eastlake. Circa 1865. Reproduced from the latter's* Hints on Household Taste.

Eastlake found an echo in Mrs. Panton, who had strong views on the subject of the dining-room and its chairs, as well as on many other aspects of furnishing. She wrote:

> For folks who require something much less expensive than even the cheapest chairs just spoken of, there are the

[1] C. L. Eastlake, *Hints on Household Taste*, 4th edition 1878, page 58. The book has been reprinted in recent years.

3s. 6d. [17½p.] rush-seated, black-framed chairs, sold by Oetzmann & Co., which are strong, artistic in appearance, and infinitely to be preferred to the chairs in the terrible 'suites', that are such a temptation to the unwary, and to those who make that most fatal of all mistakes, and do their shopping in a hurry: than which there cannot be a greater error. I personally am very fond of these simple chairs, with rush seats, if the frames are stained 'Liberty green'. In that case all the furniture should be stained green to harmonise. . . . [1]

The simple 'Art Furniture' gained wide support from the public. Once this had taken place it could be manufactured in

[1] J. E. Panton, *From Kitchen to Garret: Hints for Young Householders*, revised edition 1893, page 73.

Left, *Fig. 194: Sideboard exhibited at the Paris International Exhibition of 1867 by Holland and Sons of London.* **Below,** *Fig. 195: Drawing-room furniture advertised by Maple's in 1887.*

NOVELTIES in Fancy DRAWING-ROOM FURNITURE, such as Brackets, Occasional Tables, Settees, Pouffe Ottomans, Gossip-Chairs, Card-Tables, Easels, Pedestals, Cabinets, Screens, Writing-Tables, &c., at most Moderate Prices. Special Catalogue. MAPLE and CO., London Paris, and Smyrna.

THE BUXTON SUITE, 24 Guineas.

The BUXTON Drawing-room Suite, comprising a comfortable Couch, two Easy and six Occasional Chairs, upholstered in fashionable Tapestry or Velvet; a handsome Cabinet, with carved panels to lower doors, and cupboard above inclosed by bevelled plate-glass doors; elegant Overmantel, with seven bevelled silvered plates; and Octagonal Centre Table. Walnut or Ebonised, 24 Guineas.

quantity and could be produced very much more cheaply than elaborately inlaid or carved articles. Much of it was given an ebonised finish relieved by thin lines incised and picked out in gold, while recessed panels bore cheaply-produced coloured decoration aping the painting used earlier by Morris. Typical of tens of thousands of such pieces is the 'Handsome Early English Ebonised Cabinet, Richly Decorated', which was readily available in 1884 in three widths: 4 ft. at £7·35, 4 ft. 6 in. at £10·50, and 5 ft. at £13·65. At about the same date it was possible to purchase a complete drawing-room suite, including a seven-plate overmantel mirror, with a choice of ebonised or walnut finish, for £25·20 (Fig. 195).

More sophisticated and more wealthy buyers would perhaps have selected furniture of the type shown in Fig. 191 which formed an illustration to Mrs. Orrinsmith's book, *The Drawing Room*, published in 1878. Here can be seen clear signs of the interest in the Far East which spread across Europe and America in the last decades of the 19th Century. Chinese porcelain and everything Japanese were studied and collected, and few fashionable homes did not boast something from at least one of the two distant lands. The corner of the room illustrated contains its fair share, not only is there a display of porcelain but the lines of the writing-table below the scroll-painting on the left are an anglicised version of Japanese. The table is like the work of E. W. Godwin, a man who designed both houses and furniture, and was among the first in England to be inspired by Japan.

In the 1880's the Orient was everywhere: Whistler had been in court over his action against Ruskin for libel. This was after the latter had accused him of 'flinging a pot of paint in the public's face' with one of his Japanese-style *Nocturnes*, and the proceedings filled the Press. K'ang Hsi period underglaze-blue porcelain, the so-called

Nankin, was the rage, and hawthorn-pattern ginger jars were fetching hundreds of pounds apiece; an astronomical price for wares that had been ignored since the 18th Century.

Mrs. Panton advocated fashionable touches, and suggested the desirability of having a few potted plants standing on small tables in the morning-room, 'for nothing gives so Oriental or artistic

*Left, Fig. 196: Chairs designed by Charles Rennie Mackintosh for the Willow Tea Rooms, Sauchiehall Street, Glasgow. Circa 1904. (Sotheby's.) **Below,** Fig. 197: Mahogany and beechwood music cabinet known as 'The Charm of Orpheus'. Designed by W. A. S. Benson and made by C. Rogers, the incised decoration designed by Heywood Sumner and executed by G. H. Walton. Shown at the Arts and Crafts Exhibition, 1889. Width 86·4 cm. (National Museum, Stockholm; photograph Christie's.)*

appearance as plenty of plants, ferns, and palms. . . .' For footstools in the same room she recommends 'the square Oriental-looking ones, at 4s. 6d. [22½p.] purchasable at Shoolbred's. To extend the theme, she tells Angelina, her fictional and infinitely patient protegée:

> Brackets are very useful for corners, and I especially recommend the bamboo brackets to be bought at Liberty's.

Below, *Fig. 198: Cabinet of oak inlaid with chequered bands, made for Ernest Gimson by P. Waals to a design of Sidney Barnsley. Circa 1903; width 117 cm.* **Right,** *Fig. 199: Rosewood chair with inlaid ivory ornament, part of a suite made by Brew and Company, of London, in 1886. (Both from Temple Newsam House, Yorkshire: Leeds City Art Gallery.)*

They are so cheap and light-looking, and hold odds and ends of china so nicely, and . . . quite a grand effect can be obtained by making a bracket the centre of a scheme of decoration, elaborated from Japanese fans that can surround the bracket like a halo, sending out branches or beams of colour from such a centre in all directions, in a manner invaluable to those who have no other means of decorating their walls.[1]

IN 1886 there came to a head one of the periodic revolts against the Royal Academy and its preference for paintings, with sculpture and other art forms being given a subsidiary place. As a result, a new group was formed, called the Arts and Crafts Exhibition Society, with William Morris and Edward Burne-Jones on the committee and with Walter Crane, the artist, as chairman. Its aim was 'to help the conscious cultivation of art and to interest the public in it', and the first of its annual exhibitions was held in Regent Street in 1888. Like Morris, quite a few of the members of the Society could afford to flirt with socialist views, which perhaps did not quite accord with the high prices they had to charge for their work. Their furniture and other articles were original in conception, well made, but costly to produce. A side of this political bias was, however, to be seen in the practice of naming the actual designer and executant of each object displayed, instead of showing it under the name of a wholesale or retail firm. This allowed the creator and craftsman to receive their due share of praise or blame, as well as inducing a measure of merited self-respect. As was written at the time:

> The Arts and Crafts Exhibitions ought to mark progress, and should be

---

[1] E. J. Panton, op. cit., page 99.

thoroughly representative of all the virile work of the day. They have done immense good, because these shows educate the public and make them interested in craftsmanship. One solicitor friend when he came to furnish his house, tried, as far as was possible, to have things made for him. He desired to be brought into contact with the worker instead of going to some big emporium. Think how much more valuable, because of their personality, our surroundings would be to us if they vividly brought before us the egos of so many workers instead of No. So-and-so in the pages of a store catalogue.[1]

A similar group to the Arts and Crafts was the Guild of Handicraft which began in London and then moved out to the more peaceful and inspiring scenery of the Cotswold Hills. There, in one of its most beautiful villages, Chipping Camden, Gloucestershire, the Guild flourished. Oak was their chosen medium, carefully finished and with clean lines, as it was with the

[1] Fred Miller, *The Training of a Craftsman*, 1898, page 237.

Left, *Fig. 200: Satinwood drawing-room chair, made by Wright and Mansfield. Circa 1870; height 90 cm. (Private collection.)*
Below, *Fig. 201: Writing table of amboyna inlaid with ivory and various woods, and ornamented with gilt carving. Believed to have been at Osborne House, Isle of Wight, and to have been made by Holland and Sons. Circa 1865; width 96·5 cm. (Temple Newsam House, Yorkshire: Leeds City Art Gallery.)*

Above, *Fig. 202: Printed label on the frame of the chair in Fig. 200.*

Right, *Fig. 203: Mahogany armchair in the Hepplewhite style, made by Wright and Mansfield. Circa 1870. (Sotheby's.)*

workshop established at Cirencester, some 25 miles distant, by Sidney and Ernest Barnsley with Ernest Gimson. The style of furniture from the Cotswolds is typified by the corner cabinet in Fig. 198, designed just after the turn of the century by Sidney Barnsley and made for Gimson.

THE 1890's saw the spread of a fresh style, known variously as 'Anglo-French', 'Quaint', and 'Art Nouveau'. The names of Charles Rennie Mackintosh, of Glasgow, and C. F. A. Voysey, of London, both of whom were primarily architects, are linked with the style, which was at first more appreciated in Germany and other countries before it became commercialised in England and every home possessed examples of it.

Features of Art Nouveau are the excessively tall backs which re-appeared on chairs after an interval of 200 years, and the legs of chairs and tables which were often 'thin to the point of being spindly and apparently, if not actually, unsafe'.[1] A small amount of inlay was used, plaques of beaten copper or pewter were applied to relieve plain surfaces, and wrought-iron was formed into large strap hinges with fancy terminals. Tulip- and heart-shapes were ubiquitous as motifs, and together

[1] Elizabeth Aslin, op. cit., page 75.

Above, *Fig. 204: Inlaid satinwood display cabinet in the manner of Thomas Sheraton.* Circa 1870; width 249 cm. *(Bearnes & Waycotts.)*

Right, *Plate 32: Marble-topped chest of drawers with simulated bamboo mouldings.* Circa 1880; width 81 cm. *(Private collection.)*

with the whiplash curve ushered in the 20th Century.

Despite the success of the Arts and Crafts movement in its advocacy of plain oak furniture and no nonsense, there was a continued demand for pieces in what Eastlake termed 'the traditions of the Louis XIV period'. He admitted magniloquently that

> that school of decorative art, bad and vicious in principles as it was, had a certain air of luxury and grandeur about it which was due to elaboration of detail and richness of material.[1]

A restrained example of what he wrote about is illustrated in Fig. 199. The writing-table is veneered with amboyna, a West Indian wood with innumerable small curly markings like burr walnut, the inlaid lines

are of ebony and ivory and the carving on the legs and stretcher is gilt. It is thought to have come from Osborne House, Isle of Wight, an estate purchased by Queen Victoria in 1845. Furniture for Osborne and other Royal residences was supplied throughout the 19th Century by Holland and Sons, of Mount Street, and it is probable that they made this piece. It certainly has the quality of finish associated with documented examples of the firm's work.

Just as some of the restrained and homely oak furniture duly influenced the design of that made in the 20th Century, so did some of the more richly decorated pieces presage later styles. At a glance the chair in Fig. 199 might be labelled 'Edwardian', but in fact it was made in 1886 when Edward VII was still Prince of Wales and not due to succeed to the monarchy for 15 years. The chair does not look a very practical article, but like many of its successors it was not made for serious use. While so many of the true Edwardian chairs of the type did no more than occupy the seldom-used drawing room, this one formed part of a suite made for a special occasion: it was provided for the Princess of Wales, later Queen Alexandra, at the Colonial and Indian Exhibition, held at South Kensington.

In the 19th Century there was no general prejudice against owning a well-made copy of an important painting or piece of furniture; consequently many items in Royal or other ownership that could not be bought were carefully reproduced. In furniture, this was confined to pieces of 18th-Century French make, and while many of the copies were made in Paris and elsewhere over the Channel, similar work was also executed in London and a number of cabinet-makers specialised in it. They included John Webb, of Bond Street, who

---

[1] C. L. Eastlake, op. cit., page 55

made two copies of a Boulle writing-table for the third Marquess of Hertford. One of them is now in the Wallace Collection, and is seen to differ from its prototype in bearing the coat of arms and crest of the Marquess in place of those of the original owner, the Elector of Bavaria.[1]

Lord Hertford also gained the permission of Queen Victoria to have copies made of some of the Royal furniture, which had been seen by the public at an important display of old furniture held at Gore House, Knightsbridge, in 1843. The Queen was also prominent among those who loaned important works of art to the newly-formed Museum of Ornamental Art when it was opened in 1852 at Marlborough House.

As the years passed there was an increasing interest shown in many of the 18th-Century English styles. The 1867 Paris International Exhibition included a large satinwood cabinet inset with Wedgwood plaques and surmounted by three Wedgwood vases mounted in gilt metal, which earned much praise for its makers, the London firm of Wright and Mansfield.[2] Its success was followed by further essays in the same quasi-neo-classical style, and by other pastiches in the manner of Chippendale and his followers. The firm was in existence from about 1860 to 1886, and they usually stamped their name on the top of a drawer-front or somewhere else where it may be seen without difficulty. Their work was a symptom of the fresh attention that began to be paid to true 18th-Century pieces, which were being collected after having been ignored for the best part of 100 years. Introducing his mother's *Journals*, Montague Guest wrote of collecting as he recalled it in about 1860:

> . . . in regard to English furniture many people were turning out their fine old examples, which were not appreciated, or in many cases not thought worth repairing, for a more modern kind, and the old brokers' shops were teeming with the most glorious and beautiful specimens of the earlier periods, which could be obtained for almost nothing. The name of Chippendale was hardly known, while those of Sheraton, Hepplewhite, Adam, etc., which to-day [1911] are upon everybody's tongue, were then absolutely unknown.[3]

Since those days the fever of collecting has remained unabated, and there is every indication that the achievements of English cabinet-makers, known by name or anonymous, will never again be neglected.

---

[1] F. J. B. Watson, *Wallace Collection Catalogues: Furniture*, 1956, page 237.

[2] The cabinet is in the Victoria and Albert Museum. It is illustrated in Simon Jervis, *Victorian Furniture*, 1968, plate 52.

[3] *Lady Charlotte Schreiber's Journals*, ed. Montague Guest, 2 vols., vol. I, page xxviii.

INDEX

All references are to page numbers, those to the text in roman type and to the illustrations in *italic*.

Thus I resolve: Look now who will hereon.
My work is past and all my care is gone.
John Guillim (1565–1621)